GW01453085

LOONEY AND GOONEY GAMBOLING

The Ruminations of a Curmudgeon

Thomas F. Coon

MINERVA PUBLISHING CO.
MIAMI
LONDON   RIO DE JANEIRO   NEW DELHI

LOONEY AND GOONEY GAMBOLING
The Ruminations of a Curmudgeon
Copyright © Thomas F. Coon 2001

All Rights Reserved

No part of this book may be reproduced in any form
by photocopying or by any electronic or mechanical means,
including information storage or retrieval systems,
without permission in writing from both the copyright
owner and the publisher of this book.

ISBN 1 930493 33 9

First Published 2001 by
MINERVA PUBLISHING CO.
1001 Brickell Bay Drive, Suite 2310
Miami, Florida 33131

Printed for Minerva Publishing Co.

LOONEY AND GOONEY GAMBOLING

The Ruminations of a Curmudgeon

*This book is dedicated to my wife, Helene,
and my lovable daughters, Patricia Berardo,
Maureen Coon and Deborah Magnotta.*

*In addition to having great regard and love for each other, we all
enjoy a laugh – immensely. We like people who feel the same and
contribute to the fun. They are the people who make daily existence
worth living. They brighten up the classroom, the workplace, the
dining room, the parlor, and one's daily encounter with the vicissi-
tudes of personal experience. They're worth their weight in "golden
laughs".*

ACKNOWLEDGEMENTS

I want to thank the many editors, particularly those in the New York–New Jersey area, who regularly used my many short articles or letters-to-the-editors. These writings of mine are included within the covers of this book. They are the LOONEY AND GOONEY GAMBOLING mentioned in the title. I hope you will enjoy my gamboling.

Special thanks is given to a niece of mine, Barbara Stewart, who, as editor of the *Pascack Valley Community Life* newspaper, used a series of short articles and letters over a rather protracted period of time. In some respects, they kicked off my resolution to do the book and include my many letters and short articles from many other publications.

I would also like to thank my granddaughter, Kimberly Berardo, for her collaboration in the editing of the final proofs.

Bill Slossar, editor of *Twin-Boro News*, gave me the impetus to continue writing by uninterruptedly using weekly letters over a period of many months. Gail Travers, editor of *The SandPaper*, a well-regarded Jersey shore newspaper, was a boon to me. She used many letters which appeared along our famous New Jersey shore when many people were down there vacationing. When my output dipped, the *Leader Newspapers*, with Cindy Capitani as editor, impelled me to keep writing by their frequent presentation of some of my more "looney" letters.

The *North Jersey Newspapers* chain of weeklies was unalterably good to me. Beverley O'Shea of *The Suburbanite*, John A Carle and Maria Siano (excellent) of the *Suburban Trends* and Paul Rabin of the *Town News*, at an early date, were a few editors who treated me with kindness.

The *Hudson Dispatch* (with changed name to *Jersey Journal*), a long-time leading daily newspaper in New Jersey, kindly printed many letters as did such famous dailies as *The New York Post*, the

Newark Star Ledger and *The Record*. Diane Haines, the assistant publisher of the *Passaic Herald News*, assured me of frequent presentation in this leading Jersey daily newspaper. It was very pleasing to appear in *The Catholic Advocate*, the newspaper of the Archdiocese of Newark, published by Robert Dylak.

When gathering together permission-to-use letters, my old friend Malcolm A Borg, Chairman of the Board, Macromedia, was infinitely helpful when he gave blanket permission for *The Record*, *The Passaic Herald News* and the many newspapers included in his *North Jersey Newspapers* chain.

Rooters are vital in every venue of life. Some of mine were dear friends – Bill McDowell, retired County Executive of Bergen County (NJ); Dr. Conrad J Roncati, retired Court Administrator for the courts of Bergen County; Jack McCarthy, Secretary Emeritus of the New Jersey State Senate; and Walter Noone, an associate at the Waterfront Commission of New York Harbor. Bill Buckley's sister, Priscilla, former editor of the *National Review*, was helpful in ever so many ways. They had one thing in common – they all enjoyed a good laugh.

ABOUT THE AUTHOR

Tom Coon is a retired director of the Bergen County (NJ) Police and Fire Academy. Previously, he was a Supervisory Special Agent with the Office of Naval Intelligence and the Waterfront Commission of New York Harbor.

He has written several hundred articles on law enforcement and internal security, primarily as a contributing editor to the Thomas Publishing Company and the Callan Publishing Company. For many years, he wrote a column for the PBA newspaper in New Jersey. He served on the Editorial Advisory Boards of several publications, including *Police* (Charles Thomas magazine) and *Abstracts on Police Science*, published by the Criminologica Foundation of The Netherlands. He served as an adjunct instructor on General Insurance at Rutgers University, and on Police Administration at Bergen Community College. He was a president of the Society of Professional Investigators, and editor of *The Bulletin*, published by the Society.

Coon wrote the first article on Voiceprint Identification and was an advisor for Crime Inc., a Thames Television International Ltd. TV series for Public Television (and a later book based on the TV series). He is one of the real-life prototypes of the Special Agents depicted in the Academy Award winning film, *On The Waterfront*. A number of his articles have been used as training material for federal and local law enforcement agencies. In his retirement, he's known best for his humorous writings.

The Author

Contents

Introduction

Politicians, Chickens Often Share Traits   19

Familial Conversation and Political Rhetoric   21

Even Without Medal, a Hero with Honor   22

This Octogenarian is in Search of a Legend   23

Salmonella, Listeria? St. Peter Will Know   25

She's No "Lemon" in the Garden of Love   27

Today's Temptations   28

Be Mindful of Little Monopolies   29

What's Missing? One Way to Know   31

Tripping Over That Bottom Line   33

Coasting Through Life   35

In The Spotlight   37

Dumont Man Special Guest at Dedication
   Ceremonies   39

"Working Guy" Both a Laborer and a Boss   41

Lack of "Duds" Was Once Very Shocking   43

Coon Recalls Pals Were "In-betweens"   45

People Literally Bet Their Bottom Dollars   46

Reader Suggests Society "Loosen Up"   48

Tire-deflating Spikes and Non-lethal Weapons:
   First Cousins   49

Growing Old, Not an Easy Road to Travel 52

Every Market "Up" Also Has a "Down" 53

Enjoy All of Life's Delightful Moments 54

How to Gain Job Success 55

Idea of Brain Stimulators Got Him Thinking 57

Viewpoints That Differ 59

T Coon Ponders Rocker Situation 61

Poor Choice of Words 63

Going Broke Helping Worthy Causes 64

Please, Do Not Revoke My Degree 65

Things That Appear in Other Guises 67

Lofty Language Here to Stay? 69

Writer Awaits Plan for Better Teaching 71

Modern Advertising Aims to Bewilder 73

Dialogus Interruptus 75

A Calamity in Plumbing 76

What's the Bottom Line? 77

Male Kindergarten Teacher? Nah! 78

It's Cool to be Kind 79

Good Grief! Some Answers are Simple 80

Married Life Not Valued by Many Political Leaders 81

Old "Sticker Balls" Plague the Suburbs 82

Let Computer Experts Foot the Bill 84

Tom Coon Reflects on Voice, Accents 86

The Worst Could One Day Become First 87

A Bead on the Eyeball? Not Yet 88

One Thing at a Time   89

The "Last Hurrah"   90

Coon Has Questions About "NOW" Validity   91

All in Moderation   92

Worth His/Her Weight in Gold   93

Help! The Squirrels Have Taken Over Everywhere   94

Americans Show Their Gullibility at Times   96

A Fix Needed to a Cuckoo Clock   97

Drugs Are Still Out There   99

Hey, Wait Your Turn!   100

Lack of Discipline   101

Caller's Comeuppance   102

Occasional Spanks Called Okay   103

Our Wonderful Watered World   104

Yes, There is a Difference   106

The Glory Days of the Old *Garden*   107

Do Pollsters Really Exist?   111

Some Musings of a Retired "Road Warrior"   112

Writer Pondering on Status of Women   114

It's About Those Loose Bolts   115

Writer Laments Patriotism Ebb   116

Not For Nothing…   117

Joy – A Feeling that Transcends Description   118

Man Prefers to Work with Others   120

Maybe His Language Wasn't Intemperate   121

Worrying About Days and Marbles   123

Old Soldiers Never Die...   124

Senior Citizen Calls Medigap Insurers "Shills"   126

Junk in Your Lungs   128

The "Bad Boys" of American Culture   129

Voodoo Economics   131

Repulsive Correctness   132

Writer's Wondering About "Blind Faith"   133

It's the Thought   134

Believe in the "Old Rules"   135

The Times, They Are A'Changing   136

Bothered by "Snub"   138

Caught in Life's "Holding" Pattern   139

Down With the Cyberspace   141

Hard To Govern All Our Emotions   143

Legal Loan Sharking?   145

I Want To Be Told All the Negatives   147

Pondering the Prescription of Taking a
    Preponderance of Pills   149

Garbage: Where Does It All Come From?   151

Prepare to Crash   153

All in the Family   154

Reader Appreciates Women   156

Putting a Lid on Our Impulse to Hate   159

The Importance of Genes   160

They're The Unsung Heroes of Education   161

Where Angels Fear to Tread   163

What it Takes to be an American Institution   164

Downsizing: Who Is Left To Buy? 166

Next on MTV: Society Unplugged 168

New York City and DIO–3ND in WWII 169

Right Foods Cure Medical Problems 173

Is There a Lot of Hollering in The White House? 174

Excuse Me? 176

College Grad Blunders 178

Cut the Crudeness 179

There's No Secret Key Around 180

Inmates Should Ante Up 182

Is it Like "Spring Break"? 184

Is Superhighway Really a Miracle? 185

Hey, Watch Your Language! 187

Observations on Aging – The Great Equalizer 189

On Being Married To a Candidate 191

A Fat Lip? 192

Grandpa Tries to Answer Query 193

The Birds Know Real Music 194

Life is Like a Butcher's Scale 196

Important Problems 198

Specialization – Oh My Aching Tooth 199

Monday Morning Quarterbacking 201

No Time for a Full-time Job 203

It's Time To Cook Their Goose 204

Keep the Parts of the Machine Moving 206

A Simple Lesson in Painting – Navy Style 208

Living for Tomorrow – Today!   210

No Counting on Your Toes   211

Seniors Not the Only Group That Needs
    Re-Testing   212

Good Old Porky   214

The Fine Line of Office Flirtations   216

More Deadly Than the Disease   217

Nothing to Sneeze About   218

Playing Insurance Games   220

The Real Live *On The Waterfront*   224

A Grand Guessing Game   229

Gone Fishing   232

Pop's Bad Manners   234

Articulation Through Keeping One's Mouth Shut   236

Pipe Smokers Don't Get Locked Up!   237

List Of Illustrations/ Photographs

Coon and His Associates   37

Ex-Director – A Special Guest   38

Clinton "Thunked", Then He Rose To Fly Again   152

"I hate hot cereal!"   158

"I'm Running for President."   213

Sexual Harassment   215

Office Flirtations   215

Hurdles of Health Insurance Claims   221

INTRODUCTION

Some "guys" write letters to their girlfriends. Some moms write letters to their darling sons at college. "Some" who write letters to Congressmen are "nuts". Some "nuts" write letters to editors. Tom Coon writes letters to editors – but he claims he's no "nut". Most of his letters are kind of "nutty" in a light, relaxed way. They leave you chuckling to yourself. Tom's feelings are not hurt if you shake your head, laugh out aloud and say, "Tom, you're crazy" – as long as you don't say, "Tom, you're nuts." Tom has an aversion to "nuts".

POLITICIANS, CHICKENS OFTEN SHARE TRAITS

Twin-Boro News

July 5, 2000

Dear Editor,

It's my concept that we greatly enhance our chances for success in life if we strive to know everything about one subject and a little about everything. At least, aspire to the goal. I must have read this somewhere at some time and I liked it.

We are all woefully deficient in various areas. I'm a "void" when it comes to mechanical devices. My grandsons are experts.

Most city dwellers are not "so hot" when the subject pertains to farming and life on the farm. My wife was recently gazing out at the chickens from the kitchen window of her cousin's farm. She became rather perturbed about the goings on and angrily said, "I don't like that one big, nasty chicken. He's all over the yard beating up the smaller chickens."

"He's not fighting, Aunt Helene, he's mating," her young nephew dryly commented.

You must agree that we view this kind of thing with politicians much too often. It seems that many politicos have a propensity to confuse the voters. They often confuse by design. The chickens do not.

Politicians sometimes seem to be fighting each other when they're actually mating – and the other way around. They work hard at confusing the voters. Indeed, politics seems to thrive best when organized confusion abounds.

It's sometimes as confusing to know what's going on in politics as it is for a city "gal" like my wife to discern the difference between mating and the fighting of chickens. In truth, the lovey-dovey couples often behave not unlike the "combative" chickens.

Some facets of life, politics and chickens may have "genes" in common. Who knows? Facets and chickens might also have genes.

Sincerely,

T

FAMILIAL CONVERSATION AND POLITICAL RHETORIC

Herald News

July 4, 2000

The conversations of we, senior citizens, are not always profound.

My wife will say, "I need another bathroom. I don't know how we got along all these years with three girls and only one bathroom."

I'll say, "Did you say you have to take a bath? I thought I smelled something funny around here."

She'll exasperatingly respond, "What the devil are you talking about? I said, we need another bathroom."

I'll persist – "Oh, I thought you said you needed to take a bath."

She'll attempt to conclude the elucidating conversation with, "I swear, I think you've really gone totally nuts."

I tell her I like nuts, but I have to watch how many nuts I eat, since having had that diverticulitis operation.

She'll shake her head indicating "finis" to the enlightening conversation.

Would that we could terminate much of the "wind-jamming" political inanities as easily as my wife terminates our silly conversations.

EVEN WITHOUT MEDAL, A HERO WITH HONOR

The Sunday Record
June 20, 2000

"The man who dropped the bomb" (*Review & Outlook*, Page RO–1, June 18), about Paul Tibbets, the man who flew the plane that dropped the first atomic bomb over Hiroshima, was truly inspiring. How does our nation somehow reach out and get the right men for monumental government assignments whenever we have a crisis or a huge need?

One wonders why Tibbets never received a Medal of Honor. We revere our sports stars, vocalists, Hollywood stars – but we too often and disconcertingly neglect our true heroes.

I revere Tibbets because he, in all probability, saved my life (and a whole lot more). His mission also assured the survival of America and a world without totalitarian domination. The AKA 84 (*Waukesha*), my ship, was already slotted in the plans for the initial landings on Japan. Thanks to Tibbets, that design never became an eventuality. Instead, the ship became a troop transport to put the first American occupying forces at Yokosuka Naval Base and Nagasaki after hostilities ended.

Thank God for President Truman and the then young Paul Tibbets. There was a real hero, without a Medal of Honor. How could that be?

THIS OCTOGENARIAN IS IN SEARCH OF A LEGEND

Twin-Boro News

June 7, 2000

Dear Editor,

The secret to being a legend is to live so long that people ultimately and with finality say, "The old bat's a legend. He's eighty (or ninety) and we've got to admit him to the club."

Look around and you'll conclude that I'm right. Frank Sinatra died a legend, but I recall a time when Frankie was elated to hold Bing Crosby's coat for him. I remember reading that all those famous top band vocalists, with Frankie at the forefront, agreed that Bob Eberly was the greatest of them all. But Eberly died young – yesterday's mashed potatoes. George Burns was funny – though not nearly as funny as his wife and partner, Gracie, but George lived forever. He died a legend. But as comedians go, in his heyday he was never a Fred Allen, Jimmy Durante or a lot of others. He died "old as the hills", a legend.

Clark Gable, Rudolph Valentino and some others were true legends, while young and kicking, but they are gone and virtually forgotten. Monumental legends have to hang around to retain their luster.

Sir John Gielgud recently died. He was described as "the living monument to British theatrical grandeur". There were countless other plaudits heaped on old Sir John for his "magnificent performances of Hamlet, Romeo, King Lear" and others. Some effusively contended that he was the greatest Shakespearean actor of all times. A few said he was the greatest "actor" – period. "He had the mellifluous voice" – but he was also ninety-six.

Most of us recall him only as the patronizing butler, Hobson, who deigned to minister to the needs of his drunken employer, Arthur. I truly believe he became a legend, like most of the rest, because he lived so long. I'm virtually eighty-two. I'm at the legend age. I hope someone will start fishing around to decide what I can be a legend of. There must be something kicking around out there that I could be a legend of.

Sincerely,

T

SALMONELLA, LISTERIA? ST. PETER WILL KNOW

Twin-Boro News

May 31, 2000

Dear Editor,

I try to learn a bit more about a lot of things via the daily reading of the newspapers. I am, however, constantly jolted with the revelation of how dumb (as in dumb-bell) I really am.

I read in today's papers that the national government is going to require companies that churn out hot dogs and cold cuts to test their plants for the deadly "listeria bacteria". There they go meddling with my old reliable listerine, which I unalterably use every time after cleaning my teeth. Wrong! It had nothing to do with listerine. Listeria monocytogenes is less known than salmonella but it's in the same pain in the ass, neck (and stomach) family of bacteria. About 500 people died from it and 2000 were sick last year. It causes flu-like symptoms in most healthy "guys and gals" but it can be very serious to young, old or the weak. It can do really bad things to pregnant women, which impels me to contemplate that pregnant women should really live in cocoons. Day by day we learn about how many things can badly affect pregnant women.

Having once had salmonella (hallelujah), I always gulp whenever I read about some new "horribles" we can get from eggs when they are not sufficiently cooked. And I love poached eggs!

As I begin eating my precious eggs, I always say a little prayer that I won't get that hellish salmonella again. I'll now have to insert an addendum: "And please, God, don't forget listeria when I'm eating hot dogs."

I'm flabbergasted to learn about how many diverse things make us ill. At least, we know what we're dying from these days. Maybe! In the future, we may run into a colloquy that will run something like the following. "Saint Peter, I died from a bad case of salmonella." "In the pig's neck," Saint Peter will respond, "You died from listeria. You shouldn't have gulped down all those damned hot dogs."

Sincerely,

T

SHE'S NO "LEMON" IN THE GARDEN OF LOVE

Twin-Boro News

May 24, 2000

Dear Editor,

Three of the fundamental instincts of man are for self-preservation, race preservation and social esteem. In that last category – the search for esteem – we all puff a little. We brag.

I desired to do a little puffing about the "ace" I got as a wife and I facetiously inquired of her: "Were you a Ziegfeld Follies girl, a member of the cast of George White's *Scandals* or were you a Rockette?" She responded, "You have *rocks* in your head. I was a clerk in the New York Life Insurance Company."

Candor! Honesty! No bull! That's what I like about individuals and I long for in governmental officials. It is indeed lamentable that so many of our governmental officials, both parties, would blow a fuse on a "lie detector machine", when queried. Naturally – "none of my old political cronies". That's why I'm so happy that, "In the garden of love where too many lemons grow – I managed to get one of the peaches." Candid too!

She's not just a rarity. If she were in government, she'd be uniquity.

Sincerely,

T

TODAY'S TEMPTATIONS

The Star-Ledger
May 23, 2000

I commiserate with young people who have problems with what we used to call "looseness" in the sexual arena. They have a tough challenge.

In high school, my buddies and I spent hours shagging fly balls and playing two-on-two basketball. When you are running to catch a fly ball, the last thing you are thinking about is sex. When you are guarding your man in basketball, you don't have to guard against sexual misbehavior.

Today, TV, movies and advertisements constantly focus on sex. What red-blooded, all-American boy would not be tempted to lose control?

Years ago, we didn't have the overwhelming temptations that confront today's young people. I guess, we were also a little inhibited. I took one girl to the Pennsylvania Hotel's Café Rouge for a great meal and entertainment by Jimmy Dorsey, Bob Eberly and Helen O'Connor, and she didn't kiss me goodnight. I was not her steady boyfriend, she said. I was a red-blooded, all-American boy, but slow. Back then, I was not alone.

Today, boys are dating at an age when we were still throwing rocks at girls. Today, the very least they do is throw kisses.

BE MINDFUL OF LITTLE MONOPOLIES

Herald News

May 21, 2000

I had a few professors in college who kindly and seriously inquired, "Did you ever think about becoming an economist – or a psychologist?" I smiled graciously, raised my eyebrow and said to myself, "All that I'm thinking about is passing this damn course."

However, I did take a number of economics courses and one had to do with monopolies. Surprise: Bill Gates and the "railroad barons" are not the only ones who played around with the concept of monopolies.

And surprise: when touching upon the concept of monopolies, one has to deal with the "requirements" to become a lawyer, doctor, accountant, barber, police officer, etc. It's society's endeavor to guarantee that the individuals possess the high level of expertise necessary to perform these difficult tasks. But it's also the sneaky, tactful, self-serving way of "limiting the field". Monopoly? It's a kissing cousin.

The "piece of paper" is the ticket of admission to the profession. Once one gains admission, however, it should then be "all bets off", from that moment on. Competence and quality of performance should be the yardsticks of evaluation thenceforth.

No, I'm not naïve. That's the way it should work but the smart individual should be mindful that many irrelevant factors interject themselves into the ball game. Good Lord, if God made you homely as sin – study harder. If God made you witty, handsome or pretty, be careful that you don't study too little. Be ever mindful that Rabbis are not limited only to the Jewish religion. Get a couple of them. They're as valuable as a couple of degrees. In this day and age, when government is again rearing up against monopolies, we've got to guard against those little monopolies that affect us directly – and I'm not alluding to Bill Gates' company. He wants a few more millions; you just want a few more bucks.

WHAT'S MISSING? ONE WAY TO KNOW

Twin-Boro News

May 17, 2000

Dear Editor,

Did you ever reflect upon the poor individual who doesn't know what he's missing because he was never exposed to some memorable experience?

If you have never heard the song, *Midsummer In Sweden*, you don't know what you're missing. It's tranquil, captivating, beautiful and rather pleasantly haunting. It's a song written by Ray Coniff's lovely wife that he "snuck" into a Coniff record of several hit songs which included *The Shadow of Your Smile, Hello Dolly, Moon River*, etc. If you didn't purchase that particular record, "you" and most of the world were denied the joy of listening to Ann Coniff's gem – the real hit of the record.

The bachelor, who has "truly" spent all his life as a de facto bachelor, doesn't know what he missed – conjugal sex. The person who has never taken an ocean cruise has really missed one of life's joys. The "wisenheimer" kid who never gave himself a chance because he would never attend a good, light French or Italian opera has a void in his life. We're not talking about that lugubrious Wagnerian "jazz". That's an entirely different world of operatic music.

Summer at the Jersey shore both restores life and exposes one to delightful living. Envision autumn in New York (around the Radio City area)! The popular song describes it so well. If you haven't had the experiences, you don't have the slightest idea what I am talking about.

Without taking a definitive stand on Elian, it's quite evident, if or when he goes back to Cuba, he will, for a protracted period of time be painfully aware of *what he's missing*. He'll be the antithesis of the gist of my ruminations. Corn and syrup aside, it's a wonderful commentary on America.

Sincerely,

T

TRIPPING OVER THAT BOTTOM LINE

Suburban Trends

May 14, 2000

Dear Editor,

Things are not all that bad in the nation at this point in time, but let's be realistic. Things could be a lot better.

Morals have assuredly slipped. We've gotten into too darn many international rhubarbs, our economy is being increasingly challenged through the prevalence of a large undocumented work-force and we are walking on eggs in the stock exchanges. There are more.

Nobody seems to be truly getting to the crux of our problems – but I know exactly what the biggest monkey wrench in the works is. It's the "bottom line". Every minute of the day, we hear the same plaintive, omniscient conclusion whether we're talking about wars, education, the financial market, the care and feeding of Fido, politics – everything under the sun, it's the "bottom line" – over and over and over again.

It's apparent to me – but apparently to nobody else – what is going wrong. Nobody is paying attention to the predication, the whole integral basic concept, the substance – the "guts".

It's like the student who cheats on reading the assigned chapter assigned by the professor, but jumps to the usual "conclusion" that most textbooks include. He's cheating and trying to get by with a quick reading. He's another "bottom line" guy. They're so wrapped up with the "bottom line" that they are locked into the ending. It's like spelling Ohio. Remember that it's round on the ends and high in the middle – that's o-HI-o. You can't just dwell on the "o" at the end. You have to devote yourself to the entire state of the spelling. Again, recall that our problems similarly also have an o, HI and o. The high point in resolving the whole damn problem is almost always right smack in the middle.

Sincerely,

T

COASTING THROUGH LIFE

Suburban Trends
May 10, 2000

To the Editor,

Very little is written about the "lazy, indolent coast" that is endemic to most elderly people. Part of its occurrence is a natural eventuality that comes with old age. The other part is unwittingly inflicted by kind friends and family – with best of intentions.

Nations in large measure and young people, to a much lesser degree, are also vulnerable. As we grow old, we diminish in alertness, physical ability and a lot more. Family members and friends jump in to help. Very often, the help is so frequent and so overwhelming that the beneficiary lies back, more and more, and accedes to being overly taken care of.

How does it occur with young people? A new project is explained at work and "Willie-the-Ace" takes over and does it. He now knows how to do it and covets his role. Many of the other young people let the "Ace" do it.

They coast. When the teacher has a project with groups of three or four, the embryonic "Willie-the-Ace" takes over and does it. The others yawn and coast.

Nations are the same. Dare we touch upon welfare? Here again, with nations and welfare, the willing benefactors take charge and "do" for the beneficiaries. The beneficiaries, more and more, fall into the "lazy, indolent coast". Take a look at Central and South America as empirical evidence. Welfare? 'Nuff said.

My wife wonders what I'm talking about. She ingenuously contends that I've been in a "lazy, indolent coast" most of my life – particularly around the house. I tell her I always work with my brain. I'm administering. It only seems that I'm lazily and indolently coasting. You might contend it's that way with a lot of administrators you worked under.

T C

IN THE SPOTLIGHT

The Jersey Journal
May 3, 2000

Coon and His Associates

Thomas F Coon, left, formerly of North Bergen, retired director
of the Bergen County Law and Public Safety Institute, participated in the dedication of expanded facilities at the Mahwah police
and fire training academy with, from left, Jack Schmidig, Bergen
County Police Dept. chief, and former chiefs Peter Nielands and
Joel Trella.

Ex-Director – A Special Guest

Thomas F Coon of Dumont, second from right, a former director of what is now known as the Bergen County Law and Public Safety Institute, was an honored guest at a recent dedication ceremony for the expansion of the facility. With Coon are, from left, Dumont Councilman Phil Fredricks, Dumont Police Officers Joseph Rizza and Bruce Griffin and Dumont Police Chief Michael Affrunti.

DUMONT MAN SPECIAL GUEST AT DEDICATION CEREMONIES

Twin-Boro News

April 19, 2000

Thomas F Coon of Dumont was one of the honored guests at the April 7 dedication of the extensive expanded police and fire academy in Mahwah, now known as the Bergen County Law and Public Safety Institute (Police–Fire–EMS).

Coon, who often writes Letters to the Editor in the *Suburbanite*, was a director during the early years of the academy. Ronald Callisi, the current director, has increased the professional education started by the academy pioneers and has guided its extraordinary growth.

The $5 million complex expansion project doubled its size and made the institute one of the most modern in the state as well as in the entire nation.

Some of the other honored guests were state Sen. Louis F Kosco Jr.; Prosecutor William H Schmidt; County Executive William "Pat" Schuber; former County Executive William D McDowell; New Jersey State Police Superintendent Col. Carson Dunbar; Bergen County Police Chief Jack Schmidig; Bergenfield Police Chief Richard Baroch, president of the Bergen County Police Chiefs Association; Robert Herndon, president of the New Jersey Police Chiefs Association; and Assemblyman Charles "Ken" Zisa, who is also the police chief of Hackensack.

The new construction includes a large lecture auditorium, much-needed offices and a capability to make its own training videos for sale. Training in the public safety arenas to private industry will also be available.

A major feature in an extensive interactive television system, it permits students at thirty-five locations throughout the county to participate in lectures being conducted at the academy. In the future, the reach-out will, in all probability, be regional and international.

The expansion of the institution has taken place under former County Executive McDowell and the current County Executive Schuber.

"WORKING GUY" BOTH A LABORER AND A BOSS

Twin-Boro News

April 19, 2000

Dear Editor,

Joe, "the working guy", has a dilemma that's challenging his per-spective on the nation's business enterprise structure.

He's a worker and is thus a part of labor. Joe has also built up a handsome investment portfolio. He owns his own home.

Recall, the capitalistic system is comprised of land, labor, capi-tal and entrepreneurship.

Wouldn't it drive you to distraction? His union is vigorously pressing to retain all of its employee benefits in addition to obtain-ing what it deems to be a fair salary increase.

The company is dragging its feet on acceding to the demands. It's a problem between labor and a corporation. The legendary Chief Justice Marshall once described a corporation as "an artificial being, invisible, intangible and existing only in contemplation of law."

However, the mutual fund in which Joe has a more than mod-est investment holds a large block of corporate stock in a specific corporation. Joe works there!

Corporations are designed to make money in order to pay handsome dividends on their stocks. Joe is elatedly deriving greater dividend benefits from the mutual fund. He even has some stocks, which he directly purchased in his company.

Joe, in our capitalistic thriving economy, has a problem. He is a laborer for wages, but, as a stockholder, he is also a part of the "arti-ficial, invisible, intangible being" – the corporation.

There's a lot of that today. As a stockholder, he is a de jure part of ownership. Enigmatically, he is both laborer and ultimate boss.

Reminds one of the crazy old song, "*I'm My Own Grandpa!*"

Sincerely,

T

LACK OF "DUDS" WAS ONCE VERY SHOCKING

Twin-Boro News

April 12, 2000

Dear Editor,

Morals, mores, mom's admonitions on masculine propriety – it was then and now! There have been changes – extraordinary changes. Blushing is totally out.

As a twelve-year-old youth, I was a champion ice speed skater. Around that time, Ad Carter's son tried ice speed skating but did not do very well. Ad Carter was the cartoonist who drew the widely syndicated cartoon "Just Kids". It was the "Charlie Brown" of the day.

One Saturday morning, after the races were completed, Mr. Carter graciously invited the two of us to luncheon.

He took us to the Hollywood Restaurant on Broadway. The then famous Isham Jones orchestra and a review held forth. Rudy Vallee had exploded onto the scene and was appearing in a well-known restaurant across the street.

Breathtakingly beautiful girls were appearing in the Hollywood Restaurant show. The lead girl was indeed almost devoid of all "duds" – with nothing there above the hips. I couldn't believe it. I was under the belief that this was a violation of the law – but not for the restaurant.

It was all a challenge in the life of a twelve-year-old. I was striving to eat correctly, at this fancy restaurant, as I had been taught to do.

Among other things, I was struggling to keep the damn peas dignifiedly balanced on my fork. I dared not be seen sneaking a look, but the sudden cascading of the peas off my fork, into my lap did me in.

Life is perennially a thing of timing. If the referee had started his count sooner, Jack Dempsey would have knocked out Gene Tunney.

If Churchill hadn't taken over at the helm, Germany undoubtedly would have beaten England.

If it were today, I could have taken my time in nonchalantly watching and enjoying the show – while balancing the peas on my fork. Timing was my demise.

Unfortunately, we see "infinitely worse" these days on public television and the afternoon soaps.

Sincerely,

T

COON RECALLS PALS WERE "IN-BETWEENS"

Suburbanite
April 12, 2000

To the Editor,

When I was growing up, my favorite "hang-around-with" buddies were the "Mr. In-between" guys. I knew quite a few of them, though I was also tied closely to the serious athletes.

They were not the "first or second row" kids in grammar school. They were also those satisfied C-plus and B fellows in high school. Some played varsity baseball, basketball or football, but they were not the obnoxious "jocks". They all avidly played pick-up basketball, handball and shagging flies (baseball) in the park.

Some were so extraordinarily good that we inquired why the heck they didn't go out for varsity. They were totally comfortable with themselves. They really loved sports, but sports were not their "end-all" of living.

So many of this group gradually and ultimately put it into first gear, scholastically, and went on to truly majestic heights in government and private enterprise. "Mr. In-between" was quite a guy. A common denominator of this likeable group was they all had a sense of humor – one of life's requisites for success and happy living.

T C

PEOPLE LITERALLY BET THEIR BOTTOM DOLLARS

Twin-Boro News

April 5, 2000

Dear Editor,

Take a dollar and a quarter and fifty cents for the papers. Also, take a dollar out of the five for a "rub off". We daily purchase some form of lottery ticket and keep our fingers crossed.

Life has become a massive "wagering contract". People who would never ever bet on the "bangtails" now tell the men in the stationery store to take a "buck" for a quick chance at betting a winner.

It's a social malady. They're also in the stock market full blast.

People spent more money last year on legal bets than they did on groceries – in addition to something in the vicinity of $400 billion on illegal sports gambling.

There's always been a mix-up in state gambling concepts, society's genuine desires and the nation's de jure gambling laws. Newspapers publish the point spreads on college games, though it's illegal to gamble on the games. It's legal to bet on the horses at the track at the windows. But it's illegal to conveniently place your bet, in your seat, with a roving bookmaker.

For many years, we sat on bugs and wiretaps in connection with illegal gambling operations as a prelude to the big raid – and arrests. Some law enforcement "guys" took note of good tips on the wires – and quickly placed bets with illegal bookmakers. Crazy! It was a lot like insider trading on the market – manifestly wrong bet finaglers are never listening.

We used to popularly use the phrase "Bet your bottom dollar" as strong affirmation of one's conviction on topics and stances.

Today, too many people are literally betting their bottom dollars – on everything. Did somebody also mention the stock market?

Sincerely,

T

READER SUGGESTS SOCIETY "LOOSEN UP"

Suburbanite

April 5, 2000

To the Editor,

In tense family, racial, political, international, national, juvenile –
you name it – explosions, one of the primary needs when diffusing
the turbulence is to "loosen up". It's generally the overriding contribution to acceptable resolution.

Society is troubled these days by the presence of too many people who really do not endeavor to sincerely "loosen up" and
achieve happy endings. Rather than "loosen up", they adroitly
torch the flame when hard-working "firemen" are striving to put
out the unfriendly fire.

A lot of purported leaders have to be cut loose from the process
while genuine, purposeful leaders "loosen up" and channel the
stormy bitterness back to reconciliation. "Loosen up" should be
the nation's mantra of compatibility.

There's a strong affinity between understanding, compassion,
conciliation, commiseration and the ability and willingness to
"loosen up".

T C

TIRE-DEFLATING SPIKES AND NON-LETHAL WEAPONS: FIRST COUSINS

NJ Cops
April 2000

Police departments in New Jersey have been given permission to use tire-deflating devices during police pursuits. The Attorney General of New Jersey, John J Farmer recently made this pronouncement. "We believe that these tire-piercing devices can provide another tool to help police officers carry out their duty while protecting the public." It's a lot like non-lethal weapons. The public and many in the media believe it is needed. Many law enforcement officers have also yearned for some manner of doing their jobs – without a disconcerting occasional loss of innocent lives. They would like to do better.

Great focus was upon non-lethal weapons for police during the turbulent sixties. It was a time when demonstrations were very widespread. Every day brought new confrontations between the police and the demonstrators. Liability for using excessive force became a great concern of governing bodies. The social responsibility of the police to contain, but not kill, also loomed prominently as a police administration problem. Death could result from overreaction or utilization of the wrong weapon for self-defense. Suddenly, we are reading about a "beanbag gun" a non-lethal weapon for the police. Farmer's decision on the tire-deflating device apparently restored impetus to thinking in this direction.

The legal rules governing the use of non-deadly force by police turn on the question of reasonableness. Reasonableness implies that police intervention was authorized and that force was needed to accomplish a lawful police objective. Reasonableness must also be in the degree of force actually employed.

In general, deadly force is justified only if either the officer's life is in danger (that is, employing the right to self-defense), or in an attempt to make an arrest for a felony. The pervasive civil demonstrations of the sixties went on a hold basis, but police concern over non-lethal weapons goes unabated. This is because many incidents are best handled by the use of non-lethal weapons. Also, you never know when there will be a pressing need because of resurgence of large-scale civilian unrest. It is certainly not the function of the police to injure or kill demonstrators no matter how provocative they may be.

Non-lethal is a relative term. A Department of Justice publication on lethal weapons, in the past, stated, "All weapons, and a wide variety of objects that are not intended to serve as weapons, create some primary or secondary risk of death or permanent injury. The probable seriousness of their effects depends upon a number of factors, not all of which are determined by design." A Dr. Nathan Wright, in the past, advocated our becoming a "rubber bullet nation". He could envision no reason why anyone should need metal bullets – including the police. However, the bitter experiences of Northern Ireland have shown that rubber bullets can and do kill people.

The President's Commission on Law Enforcement and Administration of Justice held the view that, "The qualities that must be sought in a general purpose non-lethal weapon are almost immediate incapacitation and little risk of permanent injury to the individual who is the target." Research has been done primarily in six different categories:

1. *Kinetic Energy Weapons*: Here we have batons or nightsticks and a number of projectile weapons – such as rubber bullets.
2. *Chemical Weapons*: Chemical Mace and tear gas spring to mind.
3. *Electrical Weapons*: The electrified baton that delivers a harmful electric charge of low voltage is a prime example.
4. *Synthetic Drugs*: The dart gun heads this list.
5. *Light emissions, acoustical, and cold weapons*: Weapons have been developed that use light, sound, or cold to disorient groups or to make them uncomfortable in order to immobilize them. These include hand-held or truck-mounted high intensity

lights, which blink off and on to destroy night vision and high decibel sound projections. The water canon is a popular one.

6. *Miscellaneous:* This group includes weapons designed to mark suspects or create obstacles to movement, marking weapons, odors, fluorescent marking powders, aids for dispersing or controlling civil disorders, and a lot more.

The real need for good non-lethal weapons does not seem to diminish ever. Along these lines, the two-by-four is vital when building a house and laying cement and it's also omnipresent on the piers for pallets and shoring cargo. Instead of settling disputes with the traditional guns, the vigorous boys on the piers often utilize the trusty two-by-four as a weapon. It has a "bong" sound when used on the head. It knocks the enemy cold, as if Ali or "Rocky" Graziano had hit him. But it does not kill. A funny story – but the need for true non-lethal weapons is no laughing matter. The nation still awaits any beneficial contribution that can be made. Society seeks that "better mouse trap" in this arena from anyone who has a "Thomas Edison" proclivity.

GROWING OLD, NOT AN EASY ROAD TO TRAVEL

Twin-Boro News

March 29, 2000

Dear Editor,

This superannuated business (growing old) is not an easy road to travel.

Being around the house so much, my wife and I sometimes get into each other's hair. She forgets and I forget and we get annoyed with each other.

My wife knocked the mirror off the side of the car last week. I didn't. I stopped driving some time ago – which gave me a pass.

This morning, she told me that, with advancing age, I've gone a little "nutty". I could see that we were getting into the realm of the adjective degree of comparisons and superlatives.

I naturally rebutted. I contended that she was indeed the "nuttier" and if there were two of her, she'd be the "nuttiest" in the entire household. It takes at least three to make a superlative.

She demurred – vigorously – and then in a blasé voice inquired, "What do you want for dinner, Tom?"

I wondered about reaching out for a "food taster". You never know about these easy going, pleasant women. We're uniformly sharp, however, when we admonish legislators (all shapes and sizes) to adamantly protect our Social Security.

Sincerely,

T

EVERY MARKET "UP" ALSO HAS A "DOWN"

Twin-Boro News

March 22, 2000

Dear Editor,

> *Once I built a railroad, made it run,*
> *Made it race against time.*
> *Now I've got no railroad; my money's gone.*
> *Brother can you spare a dime?*

It was one of the Depression's sad songs. The aberrational, extreme, prolonged downside of the eternal business cycle spawned some lugubrious ballads at that time.

Despite my ancient NYU degree in banking and finance, I've not reaped the harvest of the current booming stock market. "No guts?" I'm not a gambler and the stock market is indeed a form of wagering contract that necessarily has society's approbation.

I do, however, admire many alert young people, these days, for "their" financial acumen. They are doing well in the stock market. I do hope they don't get hurt.

An integral part of our economy is that pesky business cycle. For every down, there's an up and, unfortunately, for every up there is a down. Would that the down will not be a plummet.

I hope that too many will not have to holler "Geronimo" as they parachute out of the market. The whole economy will concurrently plunge.

Sincerely,

T

ENJOY ALL OF LIFE'S DELIGHTFUL MOMENTS

Herald News
March 8, 2000

My grandson, Jarrett Magnotta, pinned his opponent in a recent high school wrestling match, in front of his mom. It was a delightful moment. We've all had them, and you know what I mean. You've had your own, I'm sure.

Kirk Triplett just recently won his first golf tournament, after eleven years of play, and he picked the prestigious Nissan Open to win where he joined such greats as Palmer, Hogan, Mangrum, Couples and others. John Daly had his moment when he won the British Open. Don Jansen finally won an Olympic gold medal in ice speed skating, and my friend Jack Shea won two of them in the same sport way back in 1932.

Dan Berardo got the gold medal at Bergen Tech. Harry Truman pulled the upset of all times in beating Tom Dewey. Joe Ciccone beat the odds in being elected Bergen County Sheriff and Pat Schuber, surprisingly, beat the popular Jerry O'Connor for Bergen County executive.

There are many forms of "delightful moments" which are either momentous events or rather ordinary to others. In whatever genre, however, we individually savor them forever. That's the thing about "delightful moments". The delight is for the moment. The remembrance is forever.

HOW TO GAIN JOB SUCCESS

Suburban Trends
March 1, 2000

To the Editor,

There are many recognized tried-and-true avenues to success on the job. Study. The degree opens many doors. Indeed, the lack of a degree "closes the door" to many professions.

When on the job, promptness is still an eye catcher with many bosses. In my younger days, lateness (two or three) could bring about termination. The same prevails with malingering (too many phony absences). There came the stern intonation: "Young man, get your hat and coat, turn in your keys and company property, and go!"

Don't ever discount the importance of neatness. It's an odd arena. A boss who is a bug on neatness can be inordinately tough and you have much to fear if you are a slob. Make yourself valuable on the job. Be there when needed. Also be the smiling, willing worker. The pleasant disposition can be the ticket up the ladder of success on just about any job. Learn the jobs of associates and the roles of those above you so that, in an emergency, you can jump in and save the day.

If all the above fail, try to weasel in and become a "drinking buddy" of the boss and his intimate friends. If he's a golfer, and you are adept at "whacking and putting" the little white ball, you're "in like Flynn". Golfing buddy... Tremendous... Don't ever forget what the Harvard professor deemed to be the best guarantee of rapid and magnetic progress up the ladder of success – marry the boss's daughter. I know of one man who did wonders via a "niece". The desperate and morally weak have been known to "shack up" with the boss. I blush to mention this avenue of progress on the job.

Never forget to say a prayer at night that the good promotion fairy will touch you with her wand. If you don't get it, don't be bitter. It was God's will – then start all over again going through all the stuff and things I mentioned above. I would hope that you will adhere to those avenues that are "morally proper".

T C

IDEA OF BRAIN STIMULATORS GOT HIM THINKING

Suburban Trends

February 16, 2000

To the Editor,

There's new and exciting news on the medical scene. Cyberonics Inc. has come up with an implanted brain stimulator. It's essentially a brain pacemaker.

It's exciting news. It's provocative stuff. I'm sold on implantations. And I'm not just referring to the plantations of flowers and bulbs, though I like them, too. I particularly and surely cherish the automatic implanted cardiac defibrillator – my own. If and when the heart decides to stop doing its job, my defibrillator says, "Not on your life," and jumps in and "zaps" the heart into renewed action.

The brain stimulator, on the other hand, is a pocket-size generator implanted in the chest with wires that snake up the neck to the vagus nerve. Every few minutes, the stimulator sends tiny electric shocks to that vital nerve which carries onward to the brain. These spaced shocks lift the mood of the troubled, severely depressed patient. It's just great for those suffering with mental depression.

It gets me thinking and envisioning. We have a batch of diversified "geniuses" on the scene such as Bill Gates and playmates who are capable of achieving mind-boggling and wondrous progress. I can only guess what might be in the offing. We'll search around on the brain stimulator with a pocket devise – a mouse. The key to excellence will be quality of one's capability to surf. Get into math proficiency and then scurry around to Trigonometry, Calculus or whatever. A good man could become an actuary or a space engineer. He could score high on the college placement test. I could balance my bank statement.

When we talk about the brain, we are not delimited to "math". There will be occasions when we have to quickly hurry over to rational thinking, mechanical calculation, quick response, wise cracking. Put that little mouse on "politics" and the guy running for office will sound like Chauncey M Depew or Bill Clinton. It's no longer Elmer Fudd. Good Lord, there is no ending to what a brain stimulator will accomplish. Einstein – you're "gone with the wind". You're yesterday's mashed potatoes.

T C

VIEWPOINTS THAT DIFFER

Herald News
February 15, 2000

When I was a young man, "many moons ago", I was disposed to see things from one side only.

As time went by, I appreciated that there are many views on virtually everything in life.

One's feelings about a political candidate are strongly conditioned by the view: Will there be a job for me or my relatives? Will I reap a governmental contract or will I derive derivative power and more?

My view about politics might even be predicated upon the convictions and preference of my parents.

Whether one shall engage in certain overall types of activity or not is profoundly affected by one's religion or lack of it – the view from the aspect of morality. Pictures by Monet, Manet and the other famous impressionistic painters have to be observed from a proper view – or you get nothing out of them.

New York City has parts that are terrible – utterly repugnant. Let's not kid a kidder.

John Rocker was not all wrong.

The skyline, however, embracing the World Trade Center, the Empire State Building and the delightful Chrysler Building, is truly beautiful. It has a calming effect aside from the aesthetic grace and charm of it all. It is superlative – when viewed from the Palisades in New Jersey.

The Rainbow Room is one of America's icons – an inanimate celebrity, an institution. The view from up there is not bad at all. The entertainment includes many of the world's excellent entertainers. I've been there.

I've also been to the Bossert Roof during WWII. The Bossert Hotel was a well-known but relatively small Brooklyn hotel that "bit the dust" in the postwar era.

It had a marvelous roof with a top society band – and a view. We looked over at Manhattan from a different perspective than New Jersey observers saw the fabulous skyline.

Each, however, was startlingly breathtaking in its own revelation. The attendees at the Rainbow Room did not have the grand and beautiful view. They were looking at it from an expensive but inferior perspective... Again, the view was the key factor.

But don't go criticizing New Jerseyans.

We have the view of the New York skyline.

New Yorkers have the city's problems, but they don't have our view.

T COON PONDERS ROCKER
SITUATION

Suburbanite

February 9, 2000

To the Editor,

How many more times are we going to read that "Rocker went off his rocker"? Keep letting him swing in the wind but, in time, we'll mawkishly commiserate with him, like we did with "Jimmy the Greek" and gentle Al Campanis. "Poor guys, we feel sorry for them" is the doleful lamentation.

Dear friends, relatives, political associates, neighbors and gatherings of distinguished personages, etc., fear not, I shall not name names. But I have heard everything the ingenuous old Rocker said over and over and over again at meetings, get-togethers, political affairs, etc. Rocker made the grievous mistake – he said it collectively, in one big ball of wax.

I've heard people smilingly inquire, "What in the world happens when Oriental women get behind a wheel?" A variation pertains to young female drivers as well.

I've heard police officers assigned to duty in New York City comment that they were happy to have their guns when traveling on the subway, even more so than when performing their duties while on the job. I felt that way when I was covering the piers.

I've heard many lament that too many of the new immigrants seem unwilling to work harder at blending in with our culture, or words to that effect. Society is legitimately concerned. Rocker was harsher. He didn't say it right. He was a little dopey.

Take it from a grandfather of two lovely Oriental grandchildren. Take it from one who was praised for fairness by the legion of black longshoremen who worked the rough and tumble piers when I was with the Waterfront Commission.

All this fuss is merely an outlet for so many of those who do not truly work at basic fairness. It makes them feel good to proclaim shock and alarm.

If anyone spit at me while pitching at a Shea baseball game, I'd thank my teammates, afterwards, if they restrained me from going after the culprit with a baseball bat. Rocker didn't make the attempt. Rocker just hasn't learned to play by "the rules of the road".

We are allowed only one hate (get angry) incident at a time. Get it, Rocker?

"Man is perennially solicitous of the forgiveness of others but is extremely parsimonious in meting it out to the other guy."

T C

POOR CHOICE OF WORDS

The Jersey Journal
January 21, 2000

William Raspberry recently wrote a column in *The Jersey Journal* in which he lamented over the too abundant use of "snitches" by law enforcement practitioners. I shudder when I hear or read the word "snitch".

Some years ago when I was writing about the field of organized crime investigations, I stated that successful results by experts in this arena was achieved via cooperation with other law enforcement units, surveillance, technical surveillance (bugs and taps), undercover operations, photography, interrogations, adroit use of intelligence sections and informants. Informants were essential. This was all before the advent of the modern computers and sophisticated technical devices. The old weapons, however, are still vital.

We, in law enforcement, had always employed the term "informant". However, thinking people in the field felt that informant carries a rather harsh connotation. The situation of a friend telling upon another springs to mind. For that reason, "source of information" became the accepted term to be utilized in lieu of informant.

Keep in mind, many, many responsible individuals discreetly furnish their vital information – without pay and with courage and the very best interests of society as the motivation.

Unfortunately, however, for many years now, I have heard young criminal investigators referring to their "snitches". Whoever came up with this repugnant term, in lieu of source of information, or just about anything else, deserves a swift kick in the backside. Retrogression, you're always lurking in the wings.

GOING BROKE HELPING WORTHY CAUSES

Suburban Trends

January 16, 2000

To the Editor,

When I retired, the requests for charitable contributions began. I was not financially wanting so I contributed. Glad to do so.

My name manifestly got around. Indeed, it seemed to circulate faster than the racing cars at the "Indianapolis 500". Pity my poor mailman. He was lopsided carrying my mail. There were Christmas cards, letters from the Salvation Army, Boys Town (in every town), Red Cross, veterans' organizations, senior citizens, politicos, adopt a child, naval reserve groups, etc., and a number of more etcs.

I started to discriminatingly ignore some. Then the adroit promotions began. A calendar was sent, cards for "every occasion", address stickers and the ultimate entrapment – a few cents pasted on the letter or real stamps on the return address envelope. How could I accept something and not send something (dough) in return?

They are all so worthy, it's hard to choose between them. I feel like poor old Gulliver in his travels around the world, when he volunteered to carry the person across the water with the "guy" wrapped around his neck and shoulders. The capricious passenger then refused to get off.

Poor Gulliver! Poor people like me! We'll go broke supporting worthy causes. We may become the "next worthy cause" imminently in need of help at the rate we're going.

T C

PLEASE, DO NOT REVOKE MY DEGREE

Town News

January 12, 2000

To the Editor,

I fervently hope there are no plans in the offing by academia for revoking of old degrees from college. I got mine in 1943 after going nights for six years.

I'm now reading that many high school graduates are finding themselves unprepared for college and the work world. The various states and colleges want the students to have three years of English, two-and-a-half years of math and two years of science. Many want the graduates to also have two years of laboratory science. Pertaining to English, they want the focus on reading tax forms and technical instructions in lieu of strictly reading literature, etc.

Good Lord, I was deficient in almost all of the above. For three years in high school, I was one of those students who lugged a book or two home, under his arm everyday; it looked good. In the fourth year, I shaped up. Now, I'm helping the grandchildren with homework and I'm not doing so "hot".

Additionally, whenever we get a devise with instructions (God help us), I call one of my high school grandchildren to do the assembling.

If those fellows with the two or three degrees after their names go trying to revoke my one precious old BS degree, I'll fight. I'll holler "ex post facto" or "grandfather's clause". I won't retest for the degree or the high school diploma. The eighth grade job is "Okay" – I think.

I bet most of these "guys" with the alphabet degrees can't put the toys together either.

T C

THINGS THAT APPEAR IN OTHER GUISES

Town News

January 5, 2000

To the Editor,

Things are not always what they seem to be. The reason is often ancillary to some pre-eminent purpose.

Health and the nation's physical fitness are concerns situated on the front burner of the public's needs. Heart specialists stress the needs for exercise and proper diet for the ultimate good of the body – the individual body and the body politic. America is sensibly aware of the importance of national health. All those rapid walkers and joggers are doing their thing early in the morning and in the evening hours as well. It should contribute to their health and the nation's total advantage.

I do, however, wonder.

Almost all of us as youths had that monumental crush on some pretty girl. We conjured up excuses for passing her house. "Maybe she'll notice me," was the fervent wish. But how many times can an individual engage in this contrived and obvious ploy of walking by the house? She hadn't noticed you for three years in the same class, a couple of rows removed.

Alas, the current need for improving the health of the nation and the individual requires all that running, over hill and dale. Better physical fitness and healthy good looks are indeed a by-product. There is a real commendable predication to keep active along these lines. But the ancillary opportunity is to do exactly what we used to do in those days gone by. Be seen. And there's nothing wrong with that.

They all run for good health, that's for sure. For some, however, the ancillary reason becomes pre-eminent. We wish them all well for health and "ancillary".

T C

LOFTY LANGUAGE HERE TO STAY?

Herald News
December 17, 1999

There's pressure afoot throughout the nation to teach lawyers and judges how to eliminate the mumbo-jumbo from their writings.

The concept is to "say and write it in English" devoid of puffed-up legalistic lingo designed to make the legal profession feel powerful and learned. As a part of this advocacy, President Clinton last year "ordered use of common, everyday words in federal documents that explain how to get a benefit or service or how to comply with an agency requirement."

Nevertheless, I don't know whether America is ready for "homogenitization" of clear, uniform and understandable language. Good Lord, the Navy is not going to easily give up "port and starboard" for plain old right and left. The "Smoking Lamp" will no longer be put out. "Make way" will have to be replaced by readily understood "Get the hell out of the way". I admit, however, that "make way" is shorter, but so what?

Can you envision those doctors "making way" in this arena? I'd hate to even ask what an Adrenocorticotrophic hormone is. I couldn't ask. I couldn't say it. "Nosey-bodies" are going to demand to know what the scribbling on the prescription forms mean and learn that *prn* merely means "as needed", from *pro re nata* (Latin), and *po* means "by mouth", from *per os* (Latin) – and on and on. Somebody is going to want them to spell it out.

Accountants and Wall Street's "legalized gamblers" have their own puffing and confusing jargon.

There are lots of other arenas in which the selected employ meaningless, complicated or obscure language with the sole purpose of impressing or confusing the masses.

Change surely never comes quickly, easily or sensibly. Recall that the Catholic Church changed the Mass. They put it in English and nobody pays attention anymore. The mystique took a nosedive. Putting it in English was a good thing but look what happened.

Be careful when you rush too headlong into making things clear and understandable. Let's face it. A lot of us enjoy being dumb but happy.

WRITER AWAITS PLAN FOR BETTER TEACHING

Suburbanite

December 15, 1999

To the Editor,

Gov. Whitman said she'd call upon New Jersey teachers to agree to an as-yet-undeveloped plan that would reward teachers for high student performance. We wait with bated breath for the developed plan.

I truly admire her for her good intentions, for I'm sure she's the epitome of sincerity and high expectations. I do, however, have a commiserate feeling for her. It's remindful of my coined maxim, "Would that our aspirations could all be realized though we know we often aspire to that which cannot be."

I was never overwhelmed by the concept of merit raises (as an administrator), for it was disconcerting that the golfing partner, the drinking buddy, the buffoon and the sycophant too often winds up as the "ace" – the lucky meritorious one. In life too, as we desire it, there is a system endemic to America called politics – for good and sometimes evil.

What, indeed, would be high performance? A home room teacher, this past year, working in partnership with a resource room teacher, inspired a grandson to like school, laugh with the teachers, achieve beyond expectations and then some. I think the only ones who really know how good the performance was are "we" – the parents and grandparents.

Some teachers are tough, and parents often sincerely do not like them because they are demanding of good performance. Such teachers are often assigned the "busters" to handle and try to get something out of them.

There are so many immeasurable factors. They are the nebulous, the fly in the ointment. The concept is good. The implementation, however, is as tough as tenure is to handle. The cure represents a danger possibly worse than the problem.

It's the kind of problem to which one tenders well wishes to all who venture into the minefield but – the "buts" loom prominently to everyone whose inquiring toes step upon the mines.

T C

MODERN ADVERTISING AIMS TO BEWILDER

Leader Newspapers, Inc.
October 7, 1999

To the Editor,

I'm eighty-one and I've slipped with a capital SLIP. First, it was physical and this is extremely disconcerting. Now there's discernible slippage "upstairs" and that's really calamitous. I frequently can't hear what people are saying and when I do hear what they're saying, I don't always really know what they're saying.

Partly, however, I think it's the fault of those darn advertising experts. The TV marketing "thing" right now is to dash onto the screen with a series of staccato one-liners. There's the first line, and I'm told that's supposed to lead one's thinking to the second line. I really don't know what the first line is saying and then the supposedly relevant second line comes on the screen but I don't comprehend the relevancy of the second line, nor the third.

Then, at the crescendo, we are revealed the name of the product that's being advertised. I bewilderingly ask my wife, "What the heck was that all about?" She responds, "Darned if I know." My sharp young grandson chimes in with "Haven't got a clue."

I think it's terrible. They're speeding me down the road of "foggy thinking" way ahead of my time. Good Lord, I long for sensible advertisements like, "Where's the beef?" or "Please pass the jelly." How about, "What this country needs is a good 'five-cent cigar'."

The old American Experience Mortality tables, which were used when calculating life insurance premiums, figured everyone was dead at the age of ninety-six. I admit we all had friends who seemed to be dead in the cerebral department from day one.

Nevertheless, these profound advertising guys are trying to speed up my decline and demise.

I'm not nearly ninety-six, I only feel like I am when I see the TV commercials.

T C

DIALOGUS INTERRUPTUS

Suburban Trends
September 8, 1999

To the Editor,

"Don't interrupt when someone else is talking," my kind and wise mother used to admonish me and my brothers. Freedom from interruption is an important facet of courtesy, but I've encountered little of it. I actually became a writer because I could never get into conversations. Interruptions were the villain.

I politely waited for my turn and when it came, someone else loudly, inevitably and immediately jumped in and interrupted me. I bridled.

I marvel at the current Barbara Walters and friends at noon (the View) and all those other gibby-gabby-blabber talk shows. On all those wind-jamming shows, the interrupters interrupt the interrupters. The most adroit man or woman (interrupter) wins. The best interrupters are invariably women. There – I said it.

My wife is naturally an exception. She's always charming and polite. It's only on rare occasions that she climbs in with a profound commentary, like, "Tom, you're talking through your hat."

T C

A CALAMITY IN PLUMBING

Suburban Trends
August 18, 1999

To the Editor,

The Hackensack Medical Center is on the threshold of becoming one of the very top medical centers in the entire nation.

It has everything, and everything in its consummation has been done magnificently. They have top doctors and every illness and affliction under the sun is manageable. The new functional hospital stands there, immediately adjacent to the large, new, beautiful building with the immediately available offices of all the skilled specialists. It's great.

They made the one monumental mistake, however, reminiscent of the "dopey plumber". He sets up a wonderful drainage system of four-, five- and six-inch pipes feeding into one big ten-inch drainpipe, which is then connected with a culminating one-inch pipe. It's a calamity in plumbing.

The one-inch pipe at the Medical Center is the parking complex. It too is a calamity.

T C

WHAT'S THE BOTTOM LINE?

Herald News
June 24, 1999

The President, governors, mayors, senators, CEOs, superintendents of schools, principals and just about everybody in positions of authority these days talk seriously, gaze severely, and then intone, "The bottom line is…"

I've kicked around for eighty-one years, rose from enlisted man to commissioned officer during World War II, went through a couple of careers, and never got to "the bottom line".

Nobody did.

We didn't even know what it was kicking around out there. I don't know how we all survived these many years without the magic and the omniscience of "the bottom line".

During the depression we were all familiar with firms going "bottom up" or "bottoming out". That was a horse of a different color – a dead horse. Today's Horatio Algers like to regularly grind out the phrase, "the bottom line". You have to know that they are profound and important if they invoke "the bottom line".

But I have misgivings that they don't know any more about the elusive "bottom line" than thee and me.

MALE KINDERGARTEN TEACHER? NAH!

Suburban Trends
May 30, 1999

I look upon teachers as a group of my favorite people, but just recently, I was disconcerted by an item in the public press. I read that a gentleman who teaches in kindergarten in Georgia was selected as the "1999 National Teacher of the Year".

He has all kinds of games that motivate kids to read and keep failure at bay. It sounds great. Maybe it and he are. But I'll take a Nancy Hutchinson or a Nancy Blackwell who gives a little hug, adroitly handles the puddle under the chair and does all kinds of things a mother tenderly does.

Let's face a fact of life. The kindergarten teacher is mostly a teaching "surrogate mother".

I don't mean to derogate our National Teacher of the Year, but I've always had misgivings about teachers who become administrators or members of educational selection boards, etc. Teachers whom I love suddenly become "aberrant" when they become administrators or experts.

I served as the Director of the Bergen County Police and Fire Academy for a period of time and have since had my own apprehensions. Did I suffer the plague of the educational administration? I hope that the police specialty was my guard against the virus.

Sincere congratulations to our National Teacher of the Year – a unique male kindergarten teacher, but I'll take my version. The first name has to be Nancy, Mary, Ann, Penelope or whatever. Anyone of the right sex and species will do. I'd want to be hugged by one of them in lieu of by an ex-marine.

IT'S COOL TO BE KIND

Suburban Trends

May 23, 1999

To the Editor,

The nation sometimes seems to yearn to fail. The little girl wondered if there is a Santa Claus and had to be reassured by the kindly editorial writer who convinced her there is. How could she harbor such doubts? It's a good thing there was a kind editorial writer kicking around.

One of the pathetic youths in Colorado recited a whole litany of great things – then capriciously demeaned them all. He seemed adverse to goodness, success, niceties and such. He yearned to be wrong and out of the mainstream. He succeeded, and then some.

It should be constantly and matter-of-factually reaffirmed that it's okay to be good, loyal to America, courteous, neat, kind, and all sorts of pleasant things. It really is. I loathe the expression, but it should be stated that "It's cool".

T C

GOOD GRIEF! SOME ANSWERS ARE SIMPLE

Suburban Trends
April 21, 1999

The nation has many useful, informative publications. They are great for research. *The World Almanac*, my twenty-nine volume encyclopedia and the "trusty" *Blue Jacket's Manual* are just a few in an abundant supply.

The nation now has the Internet. If I ever become adroit with a computer, I'll use it. But for now, one of my cherished, much appreciated reference sources is my Charlie Brown's *Cyclopedia*. It consists of fifteen little books with such diverse titles as *Your Amazing Body*, *Animals Through the Ages*, *Blast Off to Space*, *Creatures of Land and Sea* and a whole lot more.

When I help my grandchildren, I always check the Cyclopedia. One relevant, interesting interjection is inevitably discovered and winds up in the report.

My wife wonders whether it's so pleasing to me because Charlie Brown is at my current comfortable intellectual level. I tell her Charlie is at a higher level than the stars in her soap operas. On top of that, lovable Charlie's my friend – and I've never brooked derogation of a friend.

And finally, Charlie's infinitely more intelligent than a lot of people I know. I'd be happy if he were the man at the helm in Washington. You can bet, in the words of Charlie, he'd know enough not to be fooling around with any "darn old gals". He's too smart for that.

MARRIED LIFE NOT VALUED BY MANY POLITICAL LEADERS

Suburban Trends
April 7, 1999

To the Editor,

Life is reminiscent of the famous old Cyclone roller coaster at wonderful, historical Palisades Amusement Park. There are constant but regular ups and downs – and some downs are unfortunately, extremely violent.

Life regularly has its business cycles, which we read about in economic books and encounter in real life. There's a regular up and down from depression and/or recession to the happy, halcyon days of prosperity. The individual personally lives in the same manner with his/her ups and downs. I tell my children to psychologically inure themselves to the way life is now and always will be.

There are peaks of happiness that come with a new job, raises, exhilarating vacations, falling in love, marriage, graduations and ever so much more. They are indeed the peaks.

As regularly as the rise of the sun and fade of the moon, however, there will be the troughs and one has to know that they will regularly be there. We have death, illness, a draft into the army, loss of a job, demotion and the gamut of those sad periods in life.

There's many a man who has enjoyed the peak of the marriage day, but suffered the trough of "his" married life. Fortunately, nevertheless, many of us look upon marriage as one of the real lasting peaks of life. Unfortunately, our political leaders today are foisting too many troughs upon us that should not be.

T C

OLD "STICKER BALLS" PLAGUE THE SUBURBS

Suburbanite
April 7, 1999

To the Editor,

Sticker balls, they're the bane of our existence in Dumont and a large part of the Northern Valley.

They're as prevalent as the leaves in autumn. The aged late fallers – the black ones – continue to plague us even into the spring. When someone says he's going to rake leaves, that's short for leaves and a heck of a lot of sticker balls.

I really know of no great benefit that one derives from them. Acorns and pine cones have some clever and useful reasons for existing.

These sticker darlings are just there to drive us nuts. And believe me, they're a health hazard. Step on one unguardedly and off-balance and the thundering fall is unfriendly to bones and flesh. Medicare is waiting in the wings.

Rake them in the morning and you'd swear the same ones are still there at sundown, they fall so rapidly. If you don't have a shedding tree in your own backyard, you are sure to have two or three in the adjacent yards, hanging over into yours. I think these annoying balls are one of God's vehicles for constantly testing us to see if we can meet up with and handle adversity.

You might want a tree to hate when you run out of persons, places and things that you now hate. The tree that diabolically begets the little nasty balls is, I'm told, the "gum tree". We may call them gum trees but only God knows why. They yield no gum. They yield only old sticker balls. So hate the tree and its sticker balls instead of hating the black cat, Monday mornings or the snoring of your spouse. They're more deserving of your hatred.

T C

LET COMPUTER EXPERTS FOOT THE BILL

Suburban Trends

March 24, 1999

We're on the countdown to the computer world's glitch to end all glitches.

Due to the boneheadedness of all those computer geniuses, the year 2000 may enter with a bang – the bang and bust of all those computers that make all our vital machines operate while functioning on all "chips" forget about the cylinders.

Y2K is also known as the "Millennium Virus", the "Millennium Bug" or simply, the Year 2000 computer bug. I guess you know, the bright boys in computers wanted to save money – so they resorted to the two-digit shortcut. When the year 2000 arrives, unless the problem is rectified, many computers will read "00" as 1900 instead of 2000.

No big deal. Hummmph. That's your bats-in-the-belfry thought. Your alarm clock may not work, the smart bombs may bomb the chicken coop, your automatic teller machines won't work, pension systems won't pension and my automatic implanted defibrillator may stutter but not start. That will chagrin me to no end. There may be all kinds of other fun and games.

It's estimated that it will cost $300 to $600 billion smackeroos to eradicate the Y2K problem. After suits, it could climb to a trillion. I read that Bill Gates is worth about $100 billion dollars. There are a lot of other computer Horatio Algers, who made fortunes in the billions and there are slews who made skimpy old millions. Those brilliant boys who brought about the computer age can surely come up with some system of one-shot tithing by all of them – to pay for this mess.

They made the mess. Let them clean it up with a few of their spare dollar bills, stock certificates, bonds and debentures, the ones that are temporarily kicking around doing nothing.

If they fuss and holler, we should insist that they sit in rows at Nassau and Wall Streets (in stocks) with a big billboard reading, "We goofed, big time. Man-o-man, did we goof. Sorry."

TOM COON REFLECTS ON VOICE, ACCENTS

Suburbanite
March 17, 1999

I wrote the first article ever on Voiceprint Identification for Dr. Larry Kersta, its inventor. Since then we commonly see it on TV or read about some suspect whom law enforcement authorities are going to check out on Voiceprint Identification. The authorities have the recording of a voice on the telephone, which they want to link to the subject.

I've long been fascinated by "voice" and its ramifications. I recently read that there are many individuals who think that transient population, immigration from other countries and the current mass media are doing a job on our dialects and accents. They lament the "homogenization of the American landscape", feeling that the regional accents are good.

An extensive study by the National Endowment for the Humanities and Nortel Networks, however, seems to conclude that we are doing "Okay" – if one likes to hear people talk differently. Regional accents are reportedly growing even stronger in many urban areas.

I can assure you that a lot of today's conversation sounds the same to me – equally repugnant no matter where it's coming from. The famous foul epithet, which young and old use interchangeably as an adjective, noun or verb, sounds just as bad with a Boston-New England ring, the traditional Southern "speech" or the "English" that's spoken in Brooklyn.

THE WORST COULD ONE DAY BECOME FIRST

Suburban Trends

December 6, 1998

I sometimes feel that society and our educational "brain trusts" write kids off too early in life – by omniscient testing.

I was proud to be the "smartest kid in the dumb row" in grammar school and went on to become a genius. How do I know I arrived? My wife often refers to me as "the genius" and Congresswoman Marge Roukema once wrote me a letter in which she said, "Tom, I didn't know you were an expert on so many subjects."

I sometimes wonder if there is just a little sardonicism tied into these "compliments", but I quickly move on and avoid any annoying dwelling on the subject.

So, I say again, I strongly believe that some of the floundering kids eventually "become interested" and move on to unexpected heights. I'd rather be this than be the first in the class and then plunge in character and real accomplishments. I'm not naming any names. If the shoe fits, wear it.

A BEAD ON THE EYEBALL? NOT YET

Suburban Trends

December 2, 1998

Modern science is still confounded over the workings of the human eyeball. The movements of the tiny muscles do the work but nobody still knows exactly how.

There are billions of little muscles in the body pushing, pulling, lifting and doing all kinds of things that keep the old body going, but that eyeball muscle still puzzles the scientists.

At eighty, a lot of my muscles have become flabby and virtually useless. My grandson can lift heavier weights than I and my heart muscle is in deplorable shape. It needs a sophisticated machine to keep it chugging away on all cylinders. But my eye muscles seem to be okay, especially the muscle that responds to my spotting a pretty girl passing by. This muscle functions well even if I don't have my glasses on.

The Foresight Institute, a nanotechnology organization, is endeavoring to "create machines approaching the scale of the various biological examples, then build tiny robots that could assemble new materials atom by atom, or carry out microsurgery inside the body".

But they can't figure out the little old eyeball. I know mine moves fast, especially under prescribed circumstances. One of my grandsons tells me it's the same with him when he sees the teacher come back into a room in the midst of bedlam. The eyeball manifestly is a rascal. Blame it on the enigmatic, frisky little muscle that's still puzzling the researchers. It's more important at this point in time than all of the big bulging muscles belonging to recently elected Minnesota Governor Jesse Ventura.

ONE THING AT A TIME

The SandPaper
November 1998

To the Editor,

We superannuated citizens, in the main, can still think clearly, write sensibly and do many things extremely well. Though I had no desire to accompany John Glenn on his return to outer space, I still think clearly at eighty and write lucidly, constructively, thoughtfully – and grammatically correctly.

I empirically noticed that there is no diminution of ability as we grow old. Interest and desire are important. But, and it's a big "but", we have to engage in unifunction, uniconcentration and uni-everything. Foolish deviation leads to danger and too frequently, defeat. The principle is "one thing at a time", at leisurely speed. Otherwise, panic can set in. The wheels can fall off the machine.

We elderly people must face the fact that we cannot handle multiple operations at one time as we used to. Failure to be careful in this direction, from my personal standpoint, leads to mix-up and error – and mentally troubling confusion. In conversations with several people, they agree, saying they have had identical problems.

We need to "compartmentalize" – one compartment and no more, within a reasonable time frame. Otherwise, all hell can and does bust loose. I freeze, when talking, and come off a lot like our little friend, Porky the Pig.

T C

THE "LAST HURRAH"

The Post Review
November 29, 1998

John Glenn is a space hero again. He had his "Last Hurrah". He had his second trip into outer space and wants all of us senior citizens to have the pleasure of venturing into our first ride. He makes it sound like fun.

My wife contends that I should give up my seat to somebody else. She says I've already been in outer space ever since I hit sixty-five and should give somebody else a chance. I demur on the concept of my being in outer space. I think I'm still functioning on all cylinders.

My response, however, also is that I just don't want to be living dangerously at my age. If I wanted to do that, I would ride the A train in Manhattan after the sun goes down or I would take a moonlight stroll in Central Park.

I may go, nevertheless, if they let me drive.

That may kill off the whole frightening plan – particularly for those who rode with me when I was still driving an automobile. It eliminates my wife right off the bat. She said she'd opt for the outer space ride. But no "Last Hurrahs" for me.

COON HAS QUESTIONS ABOUT "NOW" VALIDITY

Suburbanite

November 18, 1998

Diogenes spent a lot of time walking around Athens searching for an honest man. Poor old Ken Starr has been searching for some time trying to get some honest answers. It's a lot like trying to wrestle a greased pig. Exercises in futility!

I've had my own search for truth and honesty. Mine pertains to NOW. Who, what, when or how is NOW? I told one of my grandsons that it's the Nutsy Organization for Women. Governor Whitman wonders a little about them too. They allow themselves to look so inane. Truly, any devotee of TV knows that NOW is the National Organization of Women. There's always someone from NOW spouting away on TV.

My wife doesn't belong, nor do my daughters, many nieces and neighbors. I've begun a canvass of my own at picnics, parties and sundry gatherings of people. "Anybody here belong to NOW?" I inquire. Deathly silence ensues. Either they don't belong or those who do belong are ashamed to admit that they do. A recent meeting of the local NOW organization created a stir. The commotion was over everyone's inability to get into a meeting place – the telephone booth in the middle of the town.

I suspect that NOW is a phantom organization. It just doesn't exist. It's a lot like polls. They exist in the mind and TV fantasy only. It's composed of a head (vociferous leaders) without a body.

ALL IN MODERATION

Herald News
November 9, 1998

One of the most important phrases of life is "just enough". Not too much and not too little. This prevails quite often in all aspects of life.

We constantly hear and read about the value of eating properly. We satisfy our hunger and need for a proper healthy diet by eating correctly. Too much food, nevertheless, is bad for our health and our appearance.

Learn to push away from the table when you have had enough.

Eating out is the same. It's one of life's profound pleasures to "eat out". When we eat out too often, however, the experience loses its attractiveness. Pleasure diminishes.

Even with cooking, the need is there. Give just a pinch of salt – but not too much. My wife recently overcooked the waffles, they were as stiff as leather. If not cooked enough, they are globby and tasteless.

When the students start getting wild, and wilder, recall the teacher's firm pronouncement, "That's just about enough of that."

Ocean cruises, exercising, conversation and even making love, are all the same. One must avoid getting too much of a good thing.

WORTH HIS/HER WEIGHT IN GOLD

The Post Review
November 8, 1998

In Business Management One and Two, many years ago at New York University, I learned all about the Principles of Organization and Management, Wage Systems and Incentives, Personnel Management and a lot more.

However, I fell into several supervisory and administrative spots along the way and learned that the academic boys didn't venture into some of the surprising and enigmatic aspects of business management. A tremendously important one was, always have a genuinely natural and funny guy/gal around the office. Big stuff – really. Business management experts seldom dwell upon such prosaic subjects – too frivolous. They don't generate a furrow in the brow.

Life is not a rose garden and surely every office I've encountered seems to fall "too often" into the category of a barberry bush.

Personnel have bitter exchanges, someone is not talking to somebody else, the atmosphere is too "managed" and there's an unhappy mode of glaring at each other. A funny individual who laughs at himself or herself and jokes over life's adversities, flare-ups and brewing battles is worth his/her weight in gold.

In my mind, he's the most underpaid person in the office – too often unappreciated, though a big factor in making the workplace a "whistle while you work" environment. He or she is indeed a contributor to a productive office.

HELP! THE SQUIRRELS HAVE TAKEN OVER EVERYWHERE

Community Life
August 26, 1998

Alfred Hitchcock came up with a classic in 1963 with his motion picture, *The Birds*. It was a *must* for everyone to see.

In the genre of all other Hitchcock films, it was chilling, to say the least. The birds increased in number and progressively became more aggressive by the hour, until they were ready to take over the town. They first started pecking at people, sort of random. Almost all of us had had an incident with a tough, brazen bluejay – so we related. "The nervy little son-of-a-gun," we said. It frightened the heck out of us, however, when Hitchcock's brazen birds started "killing people" by ganging up on them. Then they started eating through houses to get at the terrified occupants. People were the birds' menu and it gave us the shivers.

If Sir Alfred were around today, he could do a captivating film on "The Squirrels". Gosh – they've taken over the Pascack Valley and other areas as well. There are so many of them tearing around, that the small ones are getting regularly run over on the roads. I've heard that squirrels are not so good with peripheral vision. They panic while crossing streets and are taking a bad beating on the mortality tables.

The squirrels seem to be everywhere. If I go out of the front door, they scurry away. When I go out of the back door, two or three tear out from under the back porch. The trees have so many of them flying up and down that the squirrels are beginning to engage in turf wars.

They steal all the bird seed I put out and perform the most miraculous feats in getting under the porch roof to get at my intended well-hidden food. They run along the fences and they cross the electric wires like a member of those famous trapeze artists, the Walanda family.

One squirrel fell down inside my chimney, survived and ran around my cellar for five days before I was able to trap him and get rid of him. He ran around the cellar like the legendary "Road Runner" of cartoon fame. In the meantime, he knocked most of the knick-knacks off our shelves. He had my wife terrorized. My neighbor had an even worse experience. He must have gone for a "wad" of dollars before he got rid of the fuzzy little intruder.

The other day, I noticed one Mommy squirrel taking about six trips from another tree to one in my yard – carrying babies and setting up in her new nest as my new neighbor. I'm beginning to panic again. Are they the new version of *The Birds*?

My wife has started gazing out of the windows with real concern. As the man of the house, I'm trying to cloak my apprehensions. But I have my fingers crossed. I just hope nature's little furry-tailed rodents are not on the march.

AMERICANS SHOW THEIR GULLIBILITY AT TIMES

Suburban Trends
July 29, 1998

To the Editor,

Americans are no pushovers. They've traditionally been pragmatic and realists, necessarily. Here and there, however, they are amazingly gullible.

I recall my mother, one of the smartest women I have ever met, rooting and getting excited over the outcome of wrestling matches. We all remember poor old Primo Canera in his progress towards a heavyweight championship fight.

People excitedly cheered for him. Even he thought the fights were on the level, until Maxie Baer literally beat him to shreds when there was no "fix" in. Lots of blood – Primo's blood. Canera's rooters were dismayed. Bettors were not.

Did you *really* think that Billy Jean King beat Bobby Riggs in the famous tennis battle of the sexes? Bobby was a comical fellow who would give you a spot of three games on a bet and play you with oversized ski boots on. He also kept a close eye on the odds. Nobody knew what the outcome would be? Wrong. Bobby did.

Yes, there are occasions when Americans are aberrationally very gullible. Did somebody mention the Clinton case and the Clinton spin masters (aka baloney benders)?

Watch out, or they'll be trying to sell you that Cape Cod is a better place to live than Butler or Bloomingdale.

T C

A FIX NEEDED TO A CUCKOO CLOCK

Town News

July 22, 1998

To the Editor,

Like many families, we have a delightful cuckoo clock. They are cute, they keep good time and they are fun for young and old.

Friends suggest, however, that it must be annoying to have the noisy clock announcing the time during the night. "It's in the room right next to yours," they say. "Good Lord, doesn't it keep you awake? It must drive you nuts."

It doesn't bother me one iota. I actually like to hear it during the night. I enjoy my wake up, roll over and go to sleep again on three or four occasions during the night. That's the way I sleep – always have.

Often, by chance, shortly after I wake up, the cuckoo clock intones "cuckoo-cuckoo". I feel great. I know that it's two o'clock. I have several more hours in which to luxuriate in sleep. Too frequently, the cuckoo clock will "cuckoo" just once. It's a disconcerting dilemma. Is it 1 A.M.? Or is it half past "what"? The what is what I yearn to know. It's not the end-of-the-earth important, but it would contribute to the happy tranquility of the continuity of my sleep, if I only knew "what".

Bill Clinton professes to know the answers to everything – so it seems. Bill Gates seems to know a lot about everything. Why in hell can't we prevail upon these people to devise some way in which the precious cuckoo clock could call out, "one thirty" or "two thirty" or "three thirty", and so on? Hearing the one "cuckoo" really disturbs me – at night. Clinton has the uncanny ability to wiggle, waggle, weasel and weave and Gates has the ability to make billions of dollars and all kinds of things. Why can't they fix the cuckoo clock's puzzling announcements of the "half pasts"?

I love you, cuckoo clock, but I wish you could clearly call out the "half past whats".

T C

DRUGS ARE STILL OUT THERE

The Post Review

July 9, 1998

I don't know of anybody who engages in writing and doesn't enjoy reading his or her thoughts in print.

Many years ago, I did an article for law enforcement magazines, which I titled, "America Should Not Go to Pot". I was referring to the dried leaves and flowers that foolish people smoke – marijuana. It seemed that nobody was interested in putting my masterpiece into print. I gave up on it.

Sometime later, to my surprise, I was flipping through the late Guy Calissi's *Prosecutor's Digest*. Under suggested readings I saw: "America Should Not Go to Pot", by T F Coon. Somebody had used it. Shortly thereafter, I saw a similar reference in a Newark Police Department publication.

This past week, I was listening to one of those conservative vs liberal programs, which are so popular these days. The liberal "expert" was recommending that all kinds of drugs be legalized, including cocaine, heroin, Mary Jane, chemicals of the monstrosity family, inhaled, smoked, poked into the body and other "delights". Pot was an innocuous form – hard to believe.

It seems that America did indeed go to pot – in more ways than one since the time I wrote my gem of admonition. My article was put into print – but regretfully, it was not put into practice.

HEY, WAIT YOUR TURN!

Suburban Trends
June 10, 1998

Jumping over children in line to be served disturbs me. The people who brazenly do it puzzle me to no end – that they can be so unmindful of the rights and feelings of others. It doesn't even matter that the "others" are just children.

I will never jump over a child, even if the vendor insists on serving me first. I commiserate with the children. My big concern, however, is about the "jumpers". Like many people, I'm a sort of amateur psychologist. I think all those jumpers are forerunners to much of the current crowd, who follow the "me myself and I" approach to life.

These locusts are everywhere and in just about every aspect of life. They dart out of a side street in front of you. They dash in and out of lanes on the Garden State Parkway. They jump in front of old ladies in the customer lines.

They progress in business, not through good and quality performance, but rather by knocking the other fellow. Destroy the competition and do whatever it takes. They think that the "kickback" is a legitimate part of normal business.

They are much too often the only ones who can stomach the viciousness of politics, and thus, too many of the "me myself and I" crowd are running the show – a step ahead of the prosecutor.

The world is lost, right?

Not so. The good guys and gals still far outnumber the bad in politics as well as life in general. For an excellent example, in the tone of the Pharisee, look at me.

Ooooo, but I still hate those damn line jumpers.

LACK OF DISCIPLINE

The SandPaper

June 3, 1998

To the Editor,

The complaint of America is, despite our expenditure of a fortune on it, "What's happened to our national educational system?"

In my omniscience, with no equivocation, I'll tell you what the problem is – beyond a doubt. It's lack of discipline! But don't you dare go disciplining my son Johnny. He, for one, surely doesn't need your darn picking on him.

T C

CALLER'S COMEUPPANCE

The Star-Ledger
May 16, 1998

Those darn random telephone surveys drive me to distraction. I had one such call the other night, interrupting me, as I was about to watch a rerun of *Law and Order*.

The fellow asked if *Seinfeld* is my favorite comedy program. I said, "No, *Amos and Andy* is." He asked whether Bill Clinton is my favorite president. "Clinton?" I asked in amazement. "No, Cal Coolidge is."

He asked if Michael Jordan is my favorite athlete. I told him, "No, it's Babe Ruth, Jim Thorpe or Tommy Hitchcock." (Hitchcock was a 10-goal polo player.) I might even go for Jimmy Braddock or Eddie Arcaro.

He asked whether I would be commuting to New York City this year. I guess he thought I still work. I said I'd let him know if I have any occasion – after I check the obituaries each morning to see if I'm listed.

He said, "I think you're nuts." I replied, "No, I'm seventy-nine, nearly an octogenarian." He said, "We are not interested in religion for this survey. We'll cover that in another survey, but we won't call you."

I hope I contributed something to the survey.

OCCASIONAL SPANKS CALLED OKAY

Suburbanite
April 22, 1998

You're allowed to give an occasional spanking under a selective and intelligent formula – we are now hearing.

Some knowledgeable pediatricians have been tossing this concept around on national TV as reliable advice. It's usable on children between two and ten (if I heard correctly). It should naturally be done with the open hand, on the soft buttocks, with not enough energy or intent to hurt. Infrequent is also a key word.

It seems like common sense which most parents could have told them throughout those "don't ever spank your child" days – under any circumstances. Many of the experts and the "perfect parents" (often with a maid) will continue to shout out – "never". But one hopes that common sense will prevail.

It's going to make it tough for the social workers. They won't be disposed to lock up every mother who touches the child's backside with a gentle, persuasive, well-meaning hand. The social guys and gals will henceforth have a judgment call – "Is you is or is you ain't" a child beater? They can join the sexual harassment crowd that suddenly has a difficult time in making up its mind.

Common sense – you are so difficult to capture!

OUR WONDERFUL WATERED WORLD

Suburban Trends

March 29, 1998

To the Editor,

So there "was" water on Mars. But what about right now? If there's no water on that planet, I want no part of it. Without water, I think you will agree, life will be intolerable. We couldn't make gin or rye or beer or scotch. We couldn't even make champagne – so how are you going to toast the bride and groom?

We couldn't have ice cream or hard ice, and I could never have won a bunch of medals by showing off on skates. Pity the kids in school... no spitballs. Commiserate with the individual who exclaims, "I was so mad I could spit." We might see enhanced resorting to foul language, which is currently already afloat – and that's not good.

True, there would be favorable aspects to the dearth of water. There would be no rainouts of baseball games, picnics and outdoor wedding receptions. You can easily think of some others.

Nevertheless, it would indeed be sad. We'd have no Darlington Lake, where Bergen County residents could frolic during warm, summer months. Local residents would suffer because there would be no Dumont, Butler, Bergenfield or New Milford swim club. How could we abide the lack of delightful Long Beach Island for summer vacations at the shore?

In our minds, we can conjure up many little benefits – but let's be forthright. It would be a dismal old planet without water. Pity the poor guy who is so dumb he doesn't know enough to come in out of the rain. Like our governments, he might stumble around in muddled confusion, ad infinitum. The rain is his salvation. I don't know what would help our governments… colliding with another planet is not the answer.

T C

YES, THERE IS A DIFFERENCE

Pascack Valley Community Life
March 25, 1998

Thank God for profound and meaningful revelations. Also thank the Armed Forces. Our United States Government has redirected, confirmed and concluded – "guys" and "gals" are different.

I was deep into sports when I was young and I noticed that boys lived for sports but girls, in those days, pretty much entirely passed on participation. So I knew there was a difference. I later noticed other differences – pleasant ones. It no longer mattered that you couldn't choose a girl in the three on three basket ball game.

By the time I got into the Navy, I was well aware there is a monumental (with focus on physical) difference. I was an enlisted man for a while and had a short spell of barracks living. This really confirmed it all, beyond a doubt. I sure wouldn't want to invite any of those "guys" out for a date.

I was utterly astounded when I learned the military didn't know there's a difference and had boys and girls in the same barracks.

I'm glad they finally found out. As I said, however, I knew it all the time. That is a defect of life. We all seem to presume that the next guy knows everything we know – and it's not always so.

One just cannot presume. We should have touted the Armed Service on this one. It would have prevented a lot of fuss and finagling around.

THE GLORY DAYS OF THE OLD *GARDEN*

The Jersey Journal

February 25, 1998

Back in what has been described as the Golden Years of sport (Dempsey, Ruth, Thorpe, "Red" Grange, Tilden, Jones, Hitchcock, etc.), the nation was also in the midst of the glory days of the old Madison Square Garden at 8th Avenue and 49–50th Streets in New York City. *The Garden* was the pinnacle of sports achievement. Only the top sports events made it to *The Garden*. The nation did not have the proliferation of arenas throughout the many states of America such as we now have.

Virtually all the championship fights, the Millrose Games, wrestling, (Strangler Lewis-Londos, etc.) and many others were held there. Sidling onto the scene were tennis, college basketball and many others. An athlete "made it" when he appeared at *The Garden*. It was like playing the Palace in vaudeville. High school basketball preceded college basketball by just a little bit. It was the same with college basketball in relation to professional basketball. Ned Irish became the Czar of Basketball, and Freddy Podesta of North Bergen was later his trusted right hand. At the end of the basketball season, a select group of high school basketball teams from New York and New Jersey hit the jackpot. They were invited to play at *The Garden*. Surprisingly, ice speedskating had a relatively short prominent "life", well before tennis, college basketball and all the others.

Ice speedskating has noticeably achieved prominence in recent years because of the emergence of Eric Heiden, Don Jensen and Bonnie Blair as Olympic champions. Back in the thirties, nevertheless, ice speedskating had also reached a high plateau. Jack Shea of Lake Placid won the 500- and 1,500-meter championships in the 1932 Olympics. A New York favorite, Irving Jaffee, won the 5,000- and 10,000-meter championships. In addition, regular annual championships were held including the Silver Skates, the Middle Atlantic States Championship, Metropolitan Championships, Westchester County Championships, as well as indoor championships. On occasion, the New Jersey Championships were held. Weekly races were held at the now defunct Iceland Arena in NYC and the Ice Club, atop the old Madison Square Garden.

A feature of ice speedskating was the entertainment furnished between the periods at the old New York American Hockey Club games at *The Garden*. Bill Dwyer had pioneered ice hockey in New York City with his New York Americans in 1927. The Boston Bruins were the first hockey team in America – one year before the Americans were formed. The following year, the Madison Square Garden Corporation installed its own team, the New York Rangers.

To furnish exciting, lively entertainment at the NY American games, someone came up with the idea of staging ice speedskating races between the periods. Champion skaters were invited to take part. The most popular categories were the seniors, including Olympians such as Irv Jaffee, Allan Potts, Ray Murray, Ray Darmstadt, and the popular "Red" Casey and, in great demand, the juveniles. They were greased-lightning fast little crowd pleasers. I was one of the juveniles.

The races took place over a period of about three years. The races were closely followed and acclaimed. It was reported that some people actually attended the ice hockey games primarily to see the outstanding speedskating races.

The races were suddenly discontinued because hockey players complained that the ridges left on the ice by the frequent circling of the speedskaters caused the puck to flip as a hockey player was stick-weaving with the puck on the way to a possible goal. The Americans, shortly after, ran into rent problems with *The Garden* and ultimately were forced to fold.

Hockey games were held on Sunday, Tuesday and Thursday nights. While the ice speedskaters held the stage, between the periods at the Americans' games, Norville Baptie and Gladis Lamb alternated with Evelyn Chandler (figure skating) at the Ranger games. The Americans and Rangers shared the three-night-a-week schedule. Baptie later pioneered ice figure skating entertainment at a Chicago hotel and then brought his show to the old Hotel New Yorker. Evelyn Chandler was the first star, with Roy Shipstead, at big travelling ice shows. They paved the way for Sonja Heinie and all that followed. At the end of the regular winter season, the famous figure skaters, in those days, used to put on their own show at Iceland. The Olympians, two other little skaters, and I put on exhibitions of ice speedskating. While many athletes in those days were lucky to make it to *The Garden* once in a lifetime, I had the unique distinction of appearing at *The Garden* every week of the hockey season over the three-year period. I was there once or twice a week, depending on the Americans' and Rangers' schedules.

As a midget in 1931, the winter was poor for ice skating weather-wise. That year, however, I was the leading midget, with Woody Freese as my main competition. Only two championship events were held because of the lack of outdoor ice. Woody Freese won the Silver Skates and I, after a half-fall, wound up third. The next day at the same Central Park lake, I easily won the Metropolitan Championship. During the long season, in indoor handicap races at Iceland the midgets and juveniles skated against each other with a gold medal and five points for first place; silver medal and three points for second; and a bronze medal and one point for third. Though a midget, I won the season point trophy.

I peaked in performance as a juvenile. In 1932, Gerald Murray and I were the "scratch" skaters in the regular weekly races at Iceland. It was another horrible winter for ice skating and the Silver Skates and every outdoor championship was cancelled, with the exception of the Middle Atlantic States outdoor championship. Murray, Billy Shannon (the North American champion), and I took part in a 220-yard juvenile exhibition. The finishing order was Murray, Coon and Shannon. We then met in two New York State indoor championships. Murray won one and one was a dead heat between Murray and me. Shannon finished third in both races. The Middle Atlantic Skating Association did not have sufficient funds to send Murray and me to the North American championships, so it remains one of those "what might have been" life events.

Since the period was the Depression, I began to tend to the books in order to prepare for life and put training on hold. With advancing age and longer races, training was essential. By the time the Olympics rolled around for which I was old enough to try out, I had ceased competing.

In later life, I served as a Supervisory Special Agent with the Office of Naval Intelligence. I was then recruited to serve as a Special Agent with the Waterfront Commission of New York Harbor. Our exploits are depicted in the famous Academy Award winning film *On the Waterfront*. Old Hoboken longshoremen will recall me as the Commission special agent assigned to Hoboken during the first turbulent year of the Commission – at the very time the moving picture was being concurrently filmed. I later took over the Directorship of the Bergen County Police and Fire Academy. My short time "starring at *The Garden*" has remained vivid in my memory throughout a lifetime.

Thomas F Coon

DO POLLSTERS REALLY EXIST?

Town News

February 25, 1998

I've never been polled. Indeed, none of my friends have. It seems that finding someone who has been polled is as difficult as the mission of Diogenes, when he walked the streets of Athens with a lighted lantern searching for an honest man.

Whenever I go to a small cocktail party, I very frequently encounter some wide-eyed individual who inquires, "Has anybody here been polled? I never have been." The room jumps. The responses are of the same vintage – "Me neither," "No," "Nope," "Not me." Diogenes, we have done no better than you on our mission to find one.

Would the good readers drop me a note and let me know whether you know of anyone who has ever been polled. And, if feasible, could I get a look at the uniquity?

I wonder what he or she looks like. It has become puzzlingly fascinating. It's a lot like the man from another planet. Who the heck has really seen one? Who the heck has ever been polled? I think it's all a ploy when there is a sneaky endeavor to mold and pervert opinion.

SOME MUSINGS OF A RETIRED "ROAD WARRIOR"

Community Life

February 4, 1998

We read in the newspapers that heart, cancer and AIDS groups vie for more treatment money because these diseases are such big killers. If we are not careful, the deadly motor vehicle may supplant them all as number one.

There's now an imminent need to be more careful, courteous and free of the habit of carrying guns, knives and brass knuckles. The temptation is too great to use them when people are involved in fender benders.

The State of New Jersey and the nation are concerned. More than forty-five municipal police forces across New Jersey, along with the State Police, have been using $450,000 in federal grant money to pay for special overtime patrols that target the state's road warriors. They're after aggressive driving, speeding, weaving in and out of traffic, following too closely and lest we forget – unadulterated dumb and lousy driving.

My wife is one of the world's best drivers. She's fast when she is permitted to be, properly careful at all times and in conformity with all speed limitations and stop signs. She shakes her head in amazement at the current "Bugs Bunny driving".

First, there are a lot of old guys – my age – still driving. They're as dangerous as a drunken Barney Oldfield on the racetrack. There are the thousands of immigrants who somehow managed to get licenses to drive on the virtual equivalency of the Indianapolis Raceway. Some of them are about up to driving the little cars at the local amusement park.

Young female drivers are in a world of their own. And then

there are the nutsy, lousy drivers whom we've always had with us – like death and taxes. We used to have only "them". I'm off the road so there's one less of them; you should thank God.

Ladies and gentlemen, I admonish you. Keep those automobile and accident health insurance policies paid up. Don't ever forget the premiums on your life insurance policies.

It's dangerous living out there – "On the road again". It's "On the brink of sudden death again", every time we venture out in the old Model-T.

WRITER PONDERING ON STATUS OF WOMEN

Suburbanite

February 4, 1998

Women are police officers, soldiers, ministers and all sorts of things. They are even prizefighters. NOW and friends want "in" on everything whether it makes sense or not. They want to be priests and there is even some reference to God in the "feel good" community as "Mother".

I preferred the old system under which the mother in the family was the warmest, tenderest, wisest and most loving person in the whole wide world to the sons and daughters. God is also "Mother"! Come on now, smarten up. God is truly omniscient. He would never want to be the mother.

Bearing children, doing the wash (even with machines), cooking and hustling children to doctors, school events and sports (and a lot more) still falls like a thud upon Mom. In many families, she also performs a full-time job. All this prevails even in the families where the husband tries hard to contribute fairly.

IT'S ABOUT THOSE LOOSE BOLTS

The Press-Journal
January 29, 1998

There's good and bad, happiness and sadness, wealth and poverty and all forms of ups and downs. Life's a tottering big scale – tilting this way and tilting that way.

I heard some good news the other day. Some airline is going to put defibrillators on all their planes. Great news for people like me! I have ventricular arrhythmia. Most people don't know that many of what were described as "heart attacks" in the past years, actually had their origin in electrical heart problems within the heart – sudden crazy, rapid fibrillations. The result was instant death. When brought back to life, via a defibrillator, the person might hang around, alive, for many additional years. It happened to me. But (a big but), the defibrillator has to be immediately available.

I've been apprehensive, however, about taking long plane trips in the past. Then the good news was announced – the imminent availability of defibrillators on the planes. Hallelujah, it's an "up".

The very same afternoon that I heard about the defibrillators, however, I heard another TV announcement that planes are exploding, coming apart at the seams and crashing because workers have, on occasion, negligently left nuts, bolts and screws out of tail assemblies and other vital parts of the plane.

They'll have a defibrillator on the plane – great – but the darn plane will crash because somebody left a bolt or two or a screw out when working in the assembly process. Screw the plane, screw the defibrillator and screw the missing nuts, bolts and screws. I'll take John Madden's bus. Maybe he'll carry a defibrillator – just for me.

WRITER LAMENTS PATRIOTISM EBB

Suburbanite
January 14, 1998

To the Editor,

There is some lamentation that many of the current waves of immigrants do not seem to assimilate in the "old way".

The new arrivers, however, are wearing baggy pants, with their hats backwards and they love pizza and burgers, so they're really just like other Americans. Not really. They are apparently emulating some of the least desirable aspects of our culture, but they're falling short in the "patriotic assimilation" category. We must admit, nevertheless, that many of the American-born youths are also not doing all that great.

What's the reason? There are various reasons but one factor assuredly is the rapid dwindling of veterans' organizations. There was a time when most members of Congress had served in the Armed Forces. Today, men with war records are a distinct minority. They are the "Vanishing American".

Veterans' groups were in abundance after WWI and more so after WWII. Indeed, there was some competition between veterans' organizations after WWII. There is now a long interval between WWII (even the Korean and Vietnam wars) and today. The "sum pride" of veterans in their respective services – and the nation – is consequently in lesser degree. It is the result of the dwindling numbers. Admittedly, the very lifestyle of the nation is also changing and "loyalty" as a priority item is on the back burner.

Bet your bottom dollar, however, the trade-off in the diminution of patriotism and national pride is a bad bargain.

T C

NOT FOR NOTHING...

Suburban Trends
December 28, 1997

Advanced "alphabet soup" degrees are all over the lot these days. They're even common in local school systems. People are so smart, so advanced and so well educated these days that it's truly awe inspiring.

However, I'm occasionally flabbergasted at how little some have retained in the midst of all their educational odysseys. One of the major court cases which has reached the US Supreme Court is the Piscataway reverse-discrimination suit involving two school teachers. It's now become moot by virtue of a bizarre settlement in advance. One of the two teachers in the dispute has a Master's Degree. She was perturbed that her degree was not sufficient to totally eclipse the other teacher in their overall evaluation. She was quoted in the national press as having commented, "You don't get nothing in this world for having an advanced degree." She was not finished. She added, "You don't get nothing but a slap in the face."

I daily remind my grandchildren, "Avoid double negatives like you would avoid the plague." – "You don't get nothing. I'm not doing nothing. He didn't give me nothing." Failure to avoid the abominable trap is the kind of thing that will kill the applicant for a job in future life. "I didn't do nuthin" shatters glass.

One wonders who is currently teaching the English teachers English, when the English teachers are teaching the students English bad... ly?

JOY – A FEELING THAT TRANSCENDS DESCRIPTION

The Press-Journal

December 4, 1997

To the Editor,

Evaluations of employees leave me a little dubious and disquieted. As an old Business Administration college "guy", I shouldn't be. But I am.

Let's give evaluations to all teachers in Dumont, Bergen County, the State, the Nation and the world – and predicated upon them, give the excellent ones merit raises. Okay, but be sure you don't hurt my good old golfing buddy. Remember, he's an "Excellent", a "Superdooper" or "A-Okay" or whatever the hot shot is.

Michael J Murphy, former famous New York City Police Department Commissioner, had a brief stop with us as Executive Director with the Waterfront Commission of New York Harbor. He revered evaluations. My dear friend, Walter Noone, who didn't bow to any man, insisted that all the men in his squad were "excellent", and he didn't care where Mike came from, what prestigious spot he was being lined up for – and what his desires were. Walter had his convictions. He'd take on the Pope or the President if it was deemed necessary. The evaluation plan went the way of all flesh.

On a happy note, the President of the United States was always deemed to be the excellent role model of the nation. Recall Washington, Lincoln, Teddy Roosevelt, "Ike" and some others. In today's scenario, the nation should rejoice. So many can revel in the thought that they are "excellent" predicated upon the nation's role model of the day. Life has a way of working things out beautifully and happily.

Joy – it's that pleasant feeling that transcends description.

T C

MAN PREFERS TO WORK WITH OTHERS

Suburbanite
November 26, 1997

Man is a gregarious animal – particularly when required to perform arduous or rather undesirable work.

Painting a room or two in the house – alone – becomes a long, tedious, bothersome job. It's the same with raking leaves in the fall. Put together a small crew of two, three or four and it's usually transformed into fun. There's opportunity for light conversation, bantering and a proper degree of "horsing around". It becomes a heck of a lot more tolerable.

Usually, a couple of candidates go from door to door as a team when campaigning for political office. Sometimes, we see the single candidate trudging about in all his loneliness.

The reception, also, is sometimes crudely negative. That's why I try to give courteous attention to the candidate as he recites his few minutes of campaign persuasion whether I agree with him or not.

MAYBE HIS LANGUAGE WASN'T INTEMPERATE

Suburban Trends

November 16, 1997

America was troublesomely jolted into awareness of the nation's total inadequacy in the intelligence arena prior to WWII. Naval Intelligence officers clandestinely provided meager funds in the pre-WWII days to work upon the science and mechanics of breaking secret codes. It enabled us to win the Battle of Midway and WWII in the Pacific.

Unsung heroes performed similarly, at a great risk to their careers.

Responsible individuals like "Wild Bill" Donavan, head of the Office of Strategic Services during WWII and President Franklin D Roosevelt (among others) vowed, "never again". They worked feverishly and successfully in having the CIA formed. It was nothing new. England had, historically, had an agency of this type. We had been stupid in the past.

Former President George Bush recently gave an address in which he referred to CIA critics (many of whom are working for the abolishment of the CIA) as "nuts".

He might have employed more genteel language. He might have said their criticism is "ill thought out". "It's excessive", would have been fine.

"The highly critical analysis by some zealots of the press and some members of Congressional Committee reflect a frightening lack of cognizance of classified information and its life-or-death importance to America", would have been right on target.

He might have warned against the nation's falling back into a vulnerable state such as prevailed prior to WWII. He might have utilized various other phraseologies in his critique.

In retrospect, possibly he did just fine with his cryptic description. It says a lot in a little package. They are a bunch of "nuts". A capital "N" to nuts might be more appropriate.

WORRYING ABOUT DAYS AND MARBLES

The Press-Journal
November 13, 1997

It seems as if we are in a constant state of "How many days until".

It used to be, "How many days until school vacation?" Then it was (mournfully), "How many days before vacation is over?" Next, we went through, "How many days until graduation?"

Will we ever forget, how many days until we get out of the Navy (Army or whatever)? How many days until vacation was as wonderful in anticipation, with work, as it was with school. There were ever so many more. And finally, how many days until retirement?

Disconcertingly, I now worry about how many days will it be while I still have my wits (and marbles) about me. My wife kiddingly tells me she thinks I'm at the "September Song" stage with this. She's only kidding about the "marbles" – I think.

OLD SOLDIERS NEVER DIE…

Suburban Trends
September 28, 1997

To the Editor,

The American Armed Forces are allegedly slipping into profound crisis – with sexual harassment as a peripheral issue. I think I would have been the epitome of what the military wants in its service.

A lot of people thought I was going to become a priest – but I never even dreamed in that direction. Get the drift? But I really wasn't a "nerd" by any stretch of the imagination. I ice skated as a young champion in Madison Square Garden and I literally lived for sports. I was busy. I sure loved pretty women and later, cheekily asked the best-looking girls for dates – homely little cuss that I was. They surprised me. They almost all accepted. In later life, some of them, in retrospect, said they wondered, "What is there about this little so-and-so that all those pretty girls go out with him?" They apparently accepted, thinking they were in the company of something special, different.

I thought a great date was to get a kiss good night.

Ultimately, I took one of those pretty girls out, kissed her good night and went on to marry her.

I guess I'd be perfect for what the American Armed Forces apparently desire today – someone who is dumb-but-happy in the sex arena – and acts in a manner that one would think he aspired to be a priest. As I said, I really didn't and you can bet your bottom dollar my shipmates didn't. I guess most armed forces "guys" are the same today, but they are getting all kinds of flak, poor guys. We were all considered normal in the days of the Big War – many "precociously more normal than I". I closed fast, however, in the

124

homestretch.

I'd still be "Okay" in the modern day's armed forces. Like old Jimmy Carter, we'd be thinking a lot. And so far, they're not locking them up for thinking.

T C

SENIOR CITIZEN CALLS MEDIGAP INSURERS "SHILLS"

The Press-Journal

August 21, 1997

If you are a senior citizen, as I am, you are swamped by mail intended for you and your age group. Almost daily, at least one piece of sales material arrives urging the recipient to sign up, forthwith, for MediGap insurance.

It's the coverage that makes up the difference between what Medicare pays in indemnification in connection with a claim for a specific illness and what the medical supplier (hospital, doctor, etc.) charges. Every military retirement group, fraternal organization, alumnae group, AARP, the hundreds (or thousands) of standard private health insurance companies (and then some) are trying to make a sale. It's reminiscent of the carnival huckster.

Every seeker after your business, in clarion, gold print, says, "You cannot be refused – apply immediately." In small print, they later mention that you cannot be accepted if you've had any medical problems and have been treated for them during the past twelve months. It's then an entirely different ballgame.

Pray tell, is there anybody over sixty-five who has not been treated for prostate, heart, lungs, fallen arches, fading memory or some such malady within the past twelve months? The tranquility of residing in the Englewood–Tenafly–Northern Valley area is not enough.

> So you're sixty-four and going on sixty-five
> Thank your stars you're still alive.
> You've had an illness or two or three or four,
> After sixty-five you will have a helluva lot more.

Start your car and point it straight ahead,
You'll drive to doctors as often as you go to bed.
Health insurance will pay most of those bills
It will if you get insurance from one of those shills.
Happy hunting, good luck and good health,
With coverage, they'll steal away your precious wealth.

JUNK IN YOUR LUNGS

The Post Review
August 17, 1997

Dumont, Bergen County, the state of New Jersey and the nation are all engulfed in flying dust, dirt and leaves. Where are those environmental protection "guys and gals" when we need them?

My wife and I passed a Dumont residence the other day and a fellow was busy blowing his dirt and leaves in the direction of his neighbors. The next day, I commented to my wife, "The other guy is blowing dirt, dust and leaves back in the direction of the tidy neighbor from the day before." It was all done in good spirit. Nobody was mad at anybody.

Up at the well-to-do Tenafly homes on the hill, I'm told there are at least twenty professional "cleaner uppers" – all blowing dust and dirt in the direction of everybody else. If it were like the popular old song, *Up, Up and Away*, we'd be in good shape. It's not. It's actually "Up, Up and a Mass Flow of Junk Into Your Lungs." Sing that song along with the Mamas and the Papas. Like the smog of the west coast and some of our other really badly polluted areas, there must be a nose and mouth level blanket of dust permeating the atmosphere. It's hanging there ready to be gulped in. It's not asthma you are suffering from. You're sucking in all your neighbors' dust and dirt.

THE "BAD BOYS" OF AMERICAN CULTURE

Suburban Trends
August 6, 1997

Will the new system of rating entertainment shows, together with the V-chip screening devise, handle the problem of unlimited "garbage"? Maybe not. It may actually give an imprimatur for more violent and obscene programming.

What are we going to do about it? We could look to the Congress, but realistically, TV programmers and movie makers have more clout in influencing the state of American culture than the Congress. How about the US Senate, the President, Mom and Dad, the Bible, and let's be pragmatic – the protection of the US Constitution? They seem to always come out second best when confronting Hollywood's attacks on good taste, common sense and don't laugh – family values. There are always the federal courts. Whether you liked or disliked Robert Bork when he was being considered for the US Supreme Court, objective individuals, in the main, agreed with him in his assessment that the Supreme Court, itself, has made it "practically impossible to prosecute pornography and obscenity".

The nation cherishes our communications systems whether it pertains to entertainment or news dissemination. We seem to be awed by their mission and unfettered rights. In many respects, however, they remind me of the educational system. The Superintendent of Schools is afraid of the Board of Education and the PTA; the Principal is afraid of the Superintendent and the PTA; the teacher is afraid of the Superintendent and the Principal and the PTA, but "Johnny the Bad Boy" isn't afraid of anyone. Hollywood and the communications system have become the

"Bad Boys" of American culture. They are "too big for their britches", and nobody seems to be able to handle them.

There goes that Neanderthal Tom Coon advocating censorship. Hold the phone! Case closed before you start! End of discussion!

VOODOO ECONOMICS

The Star-Ledger
July 24, 1997

I took a wad of economics courses when getting my degree at New York University. I was an honors student but really don't know "spit" about current economics. I do know the difference between a business cycle and a bicycle but the income of these current "stars" leaves me in wonder. Supply and demand? Really!

Helen Forest sang with Artie Shaw, Benny Goodman and Harry James. She's associated with delightful ballads such as *All the Things You Are, I Had the Craziest Dream Last Night, Long Ago and Far Away* and a batch more. Jo Stafford was the same. There were many others. It was a rare entertainer in past years who "made a fortune".

The other day, I heard that one of our modern-day "song shouters" yielded income of $270 million on her "recent tour". That's one tour!

There's something wacky about our economy and NYU did not furnish me with the answers to this anomaly. It's "crazy, man – crazy." More apropos: "crazy economics, man – crazy." Crazy is an understatement.

REPULSIVE CORRECTNESS

The SandPaper
July 23, 1997

The phrase has been around for quite some time but I still bridle when I hear that abomination "politically correct". I immediately think in the arena of "gutlessly vacuous", "insincere", "dishonest", "frequently immoral", "repulsive" and a lot more.

The very phrase connotes waffling; fear of being debated; a stance without conviction; wrong or not, it's safe; duplicity; absence of character; and fundamentally, the willingness to stand for nothing as an acceptable bargain for survival.

The philosophy attached to the phrase may guarantee immediate survival, but it forebodes ultimate disaster. Look no further than the military. We are disconcertingly hearing rumblings of the insidious festering. Military officers are complaining that "initiative and innovation are stifled by timid leaders overly concerned with maintaining unblemished records for promotion". There are charges that the president and the Congress are allowing US military power to become directionless and dangerously brittle.

Political correctness, a synonym for "cravenness", is a root cause. It's not just the military. National, state, county and local politics are endangered by the malady. From its own pernicious aspect, it's an infection worse than HIV.

History has shown that nations' and individuals' disposition to stand for nothing in a frantic endeavor to stand safely in place, ultimately leads to disappointment and failure. Safe havens are generally not alternatives to courage, honesty, conviction and goodness. It's difficult for me to believe that anyone perceptive enough to reside or vacation on Long Beach Island would buy the inane concept of "political correctness".

WRITER'S WONDERING ABOUT "BLIND FAITH"

Suburbanite
July 16, 1997

To the Editor,

I marvel at the blasé confidence in the American automobile drivers that's daily exhibited by the joggers, brisk walkers and bike riders as they go about their energetic pleasures. They carry out their routines in many frighteningly congested and dangerous areas with a disdainful attitude of, "Make way for me and watch out that you don't hit or splash me." I wonder about their blind faith and assurance that they'll live to see another day!

Don't they know? This is the age of the "bizarre driver" and the devil-may-care young damsel. She's a speedster – with the finger in the middle to all who challenge her ownership of the American roads. The young ladies have fat feet on their accelerators, which must put many dents in the "metal". If those two don't get the "perimeter road activists", we seventy-year-old blithe spirits may do them in – in slow but deadly motion. No matter. They'll be numbers in the mortality tables, regardless of who brings about their sudden demise. Either they're too trusting or they like to live dangerously.

T C

IT'S THE THOUGHT

The SandPaper
July 2, 1997

To the Editor,
I think the insidious creep of prices is noticed quickly by the individual in retirement. My wife is big on greeting cards. Their prices jolt me. I generally make my own.

On my wife's most recent birthday, I wrote:

> Helene is twenty-two
> No, she was born in 1922
> She surely looks like twenty-two
> It's vintage 1922. She only looks brand new.

My wife said "thanks", but regarding husbands and birthdays:

> It's important that you see
> I was born in 1923.

T C

BELIEVE IN THE "OLD RULES"

Leader Newspapers, Inc.
June 19, 1997

Dear Editor,

It's very easy, today, to be labeled a homophile if one merely says, "I don't think homosexuality is the mainstream." We used to stress that the well-rounded boy believed in God and country and one dare not burn the flag.

Now, we can't prod a batch of legislators to say it's illegal to do so. The concept used to be that any bright boy, if he worked hard at advancement, might grow up to be president. Now we promote, in large measure, on the basis of affirmative action and quotas. We might reach a point in time where we're told, "It's got to be a 'gal' for president this time around and she 'gotta' be Sioux."

We used to be constantly reminded to say our prayers. Now, we are treading on dangerous ground if we are not careful where we do our praying. "Do it surreptitiously," they say. We used to stress neatness of dress. Today, sloppiness is again in. "See that disheveled looking boy with the baggy clothing? He was voted best dressed of the class." We could go on and on.

But please don't deem me over conservative if I adhere to some of the "old rules". If we are good boys, do we still go to heaven? Or is the alternative the objective? Is Lucifer in? I'm decrepit and adverse to shoveling coal, so I hope we are still doing business in the old-fashioned way on this one: "Lucifer, shovel your own damn coal. And don't go trying to singe my wings."

Sincerely,

T

THE TIMES, THEY ARE A'CHANGING

Suburban Trends
June 15, 1997

To the Editor,

Believe me, it's much tougher living and adjusting today than it was when I was young.

We encountered a minimal number of homosexuals during WWII. In fact, Naval Intelligence investigated them under the concept that they were security risks. The Germans effectively used them in WWI. Actually, a little buddy of mine, while I was still an enlisted man early in WWII, told me some fellow had made passes at him at a NYC bar, and he immediately "cold-cocked" him. I incredulously exclaimed, "You knocked him out?" He frankly responded, "What else would you do?" Upon reflection, certainly not today.

My mother was a gentlewoman. She heard one of my brothers refer to someone as a "nigger". She quickly gathered us all together and said, "Boys, any of your friends who are black loath that word. They prefer to be called Negro. It's the kind and considerate thing to do. Do it." However, if I were to refer to someone as "Negro" today at the Yankee Stadium, I'd be the one who would be cold-cocked.

My wife was watching models in swimsuits on TV today. She asked me for my expert opinion on the models. I ingeniously said, "They all look like 'broomsticks' walking around on 'bread sticks'." She responded, "There are a few with shapely legs, which one is the best?" Without hesitation, I stated, "The third one from the right." She chidingly said, "That's a man. He's modeling swimsuits." I stood pat with my evaluation.

Things are changing rapidly and it's difficult keeping up. At my age, I have some profound concerns, aside from the skinny legs. My understanding is that it's St. Peter who will do the initial screening after my demise. I hope they don't go making changes I'm not kept abreast of. It's a tough challenge trying to make everybody happy and keep up with the rapid changes.

T C

BOTHERED BY "SNUB"

Herald News
April 25, 1997

Back in our high school days, we occasionally suffered the blow of not being invited to the "in" party with all the wheels of the moment. There was the feeling of rejection. It happened to everyone.

I must say, however, that my being totally left out on an invitation to the White House for some form of clam bake or coffee klatch has me really deflated. I've heard that everybody has been invited, including Judge Crater, Oprah, Barney, Polly Adler, "Boxcar" Willie and "TinBox" Farley, among others. Why not me?

I know I was passed up on more than one occasion because my degree read NYU (night shift) instead of Yale, Harvard, Princeton – or Oxford. But this snub tops all. How much is one expected to accept with proper grace? I admit I'm rather parsimonious, so the boys can forget any million-dollar contribution. But I'd know enough to respond if I got one of those follow-up letters asking for a little largess – $100, $50, $25, $10, $5, or other, plus my opinions.

I'd give my opinions, though my contribution would be other. But I'd surely have the good sense to ante up.

CAUGHT IN LIFE'S "HOLDING" PATTERN

Suburban News
April 15, 1997

IRS representatives are available to help you with your tax questions. "If, after reading the tax form instructions and publications, you are not sure how to fill in your return, or have a question about a notice you received from us, please call us." They say please. And I had a number – 1–800–829–1040. This was super!

I called, early in the morning, but not too early. I'm retired and I didn't want to get jammed up with all those poor guys and gals who are working for a living and would be hurrying in their calls before they fly off to work. I called, but the number was busy. It was busy again and again and again during the morning and afternoon.

Around 3:45 p.m. I got into the system. I went through the whole gamut. I punched one and got into a new series of instructions. I punched three and got into another series. They told me to punch nine. I then punched something and got those wonderful, soothing instructions to stand by. Someone would talk to me. It was like manna from Heaven.

After some waiting, with music in the background, I heard the recording, "We appreciate your patience. Please continue to hold. The next available representative will assist you as soon as possible."

In the background, I heard the delightful old musical chestnut, *Love will keep us young until the very last good bye.* That is one of my all-time favorites. Carmen Cavallaro had a beautiful recording of the song. But I kept getting the request to continue to hold – over and over and over. *Love will keep us young* came up again and again,

139

along with all the other songs. Nice music. No loud, blaring cacophony.

All of a sudden, I got a dial tone. I thought to myself, "What the heck is this?" I glanced at my wristwatch and immediately realized what had happened. It was 4:30 p.m. The guy at irs had pulled the plug on everything including, *Love will keep us young until the very last goodbye*.

I'll try again tomorrow. I hope I'll make it before April 15. Hope springs eternal in the human breast.

DOWN WITH THE CYBERSPACE

The Post Review
April 6, 1997

I still feel rather confused and stupid. I hear talk about e-mail, the Internet, software, hardware and a lot more. I generally don't know what in God's name they're talking about. I smile.

I'm seventy-eight, functioning with drugs (legal) and medical machines and doing quite well. I believe I'm lucky to be licking the American Experience Mortality Tables and still hanging around, but I hate to think I'm going to have to sign up with one of the adult education groups to learn how to fathom the computer and learn its "lingo".

I keep remembering the time when I was the Director of the Bergen County Police and Fire Academy. Being up in the hinterlands of Mahwah, we had to dispatch someone to Hackensack on payday to pick up our checks. We were all sitting around with bated breath, waiting for the pay check so that we might pay for the groceries, the bookie, the loan-shark or whatever one's priority was. Suddenly we'd get the word. "I'm stuck down here in Hackensack; the sophisticated payroll system has a bug and I don't know when I'll be back in Mahwah with the checks." Hearts fluttered.

One of the long-time employees commented, "Mr. Coon, for years we had three old ladies down in Hackensack getting out the county payroll and we never had this delay business until we went to the big, automated system."

I may still stand pat. Maybe some of the old systems will be revived and I'll know what the devil is going on. The irs has already learned a lesson – having gone to a new fangled system that didn't work. Maybe a lot more will return to tried and proven systems – like little old ladies with nimble wits and fingers. Maybe we can even restore real music.

Anyway – down with the Internet, Cyberspace and all that jazz! Perhaps – perhaps we can drag our feet a little against the wheels of progress.

HARD TO GOVERN ALL OUR EMOTIONS

Town News

March 5, 1997

To the Editor,

There are a slew of fine organizations in action these days with wonderful objectives and a design to make Mother Earth a better place in which to live. There are some smart people at the helms.

They're zeroing in upon wife battering, husband irresponsibility, failure to pay for child support, racial friction, drinking and drugs and even resolving how far southern heritage groups should go in continued display of Old South songs and symbols. There are lots more.

Nevertheless, I worry in some measure over the scope of some of their objectives. They are laboring to eradicate or harness in various emotions. Wouldn't it be wonderful if they succeed – and they manage to succeed in the right directions?

However, we are indeed playing around with emotions that are tricky to maneuver. Emotions are really familiar areas to all of us – fear, anger, hope, happiness, jealousy and those resultant feelings that happen on a day-to-day basis. Without many of these emotions, life could become a kind of nothingness. There would be no labor troubles, no triumphs, no happiness, no "exciting" political campaigns, no fights with your wife – some bad, some good. We seem to be doing a great job at eradicating laughter, which is an aspect that assuredly doesn't make me happy.

These are tough areas in which the advocates are operating because they do involve some tenuous, fragile and diverse emotions. When reigning in upon some emotions, there is the imminent danger of kicking off others that might be even worse. We've been having problems in dealing with emotions since Adam and Eve made their fateful decision. It's a difficult job, the advocates assumed, but we wish them well. There have been well-wishers in these difficult arenas since Adam and Eve blundered. We should continue to do so. But let's go easy on abolishing fun and laughter. We need them to cope with many of the bad emotions.

T C

LEGAL LOAN SHARKING?

Herald News

February 14, 1997

A friend of mine who was my partner (at that time) with the Waterfront Commission once put a provocative question to me. We were in the process of investigating various rackets that were taking place on our famous waterfront.

He asked me what racket I would get into if I were devoid of morals and wanted to make heaps of money. I rather quickly answered, the gambling arena – numbers or bookmaking. He, without hesitation and with equal alacrity, responded, "Wrong, you should get into loan-sharking." He succinctly pointed out that the return on the investment is fantastic and the operation is simple. A shark needs nothing but money and borrowers. He doesn't need an office and can pretty much run it "out of his hat". A leg-breaker, however, is essential but the mob backers can come up with one of the delightful fellows.

The money flows like rain in a spring shower. If a borrower doesn't pay on the barrelhead, the leg-breaker sidles onto the scene and persuasively talks to the tardy one. If delinquency becomes a real problem, he simply breaks the borrower's leg(s), jaw or arm(s). The offender usually offends no more. I heard of a case where the delinquent's arm was thrust into a fire. Infection set in and he lost his arm – but he was never late on payments again.

I mention this because I've come to the conclusion that the modern-day loan sharks are the plastic credit card companies. They need no leg-breaker. Who needs an animal to beat up delinquents? The law of the land, in a very real sense, serves as their leg-breaker.

Society gives this form of business enterprise its imprimatur.

It's okay. It's even more okay in some states than in others – for the credit card companies. Usury, thy middle name is plastic.

I WANT TO BE TOLD ALL THE NEGATIVES

The Jersey Journal
November 29, 1996

Like a vaudeville act, negative campaigning is again a focus of news discussion.

What is it? Most people would have difficulty defining it. The candidate who carries a lot of "baggage" is adverse to it. A little bit of censorship would please him immensely. The newspaper that wants to derogate a candidate it does not like often invokes the accusation.

In fact, they themselves are gross offenders in playing with the truth. Nobody should subscribe to vicious, dishonest campaigning.

The essence of campaigning should be concerned with the truth and relevancy of the allegations.

Negative campaigning is a catchy phrase some news savant dreamed up. We've since been reading about it ad nauseum, every time we pick up a newspaper or magazine or turn on the TV.

Campaigning for office is no different today than it was a number of years ago, when I was in the mix. I am surely interested in whether Joe Candidate stole a "hot" stove in the past. He might be disposed to steal a hot stove in the future.

I think this is relevant for consideration. Many of my friends, who are assuredly not Neanderthals, feel as I do.

Please let me know about the tax fraud, connivance, crazy political proclivities, one's attitude towards the Exclusionary Rule or whether the aspirant had been hanging out with the mob.

I'm interested in whether the candidate went from holes in his shoes to become a millionaire in a matter of years – barring having hit the lottery. I'm interested in all those negatives.

PONDERING THE PRESCRIPTION OF TAKING A PREPONDERANCE OF PILLS

Pascack Valley Community Life
November 6, 1996

"Did you take your ten-minutes-to-six pill, Tom?" My wife knows my pills by what time I take them. They actually have an assortment of exotic names such as Proscar, Lasex, Slow-K, Capeten, Mexiletine, Theo-Dur and others.

Instructions tell us that we should "Take with food"… "Take on an empty stomach"… "Take with plenty of water"… etc. The others, one can take any which way, I guess.

I get up a little before 6 A.M. to take a particular pill, which should be taken an hour before eating – or two hours after. I take that first pill, hop back in bed and take a whole batch of pills at 7 A.M. when I get up for good. They include some take-with-food ones along with some take-any-which-way pills.

One take-with-food pill is taken every eight hours. All the others fit in at six-hour intervals. The problem is, I sometimes miss the one-hour-before-meal pill (on an empty stomach) and I have to take it two hours after the meal.

This presents a problem. The two-hours-after pill (on an empty stomach) now comes at 2 P.M. and a take-with-food pill comes at 3 P.M. And Bill Clinton thinks he has problems! My medication schedule can get pretty hairy. The timing is like shooting a rocket to the moon.

The 6 P.M. pills are duck soup. The take-with-food ones and the take-any-which-way pills co-mingle in a friendly fashion and go down the hatch in one gulp.

It's a pain in the neck with the batch of assorted pills I take between 11 P.M. and midnight. One has to be taken with food. The others just tag along giving no problems to the "gulper". However, to accommodate the take-with-food medication, I find myself eating a graham cracker and some cottage cheese at that late hour.

My dear friend, Jack McCarthy, Secretary Emeritus to the NJ Senate, had season tickets for the Yankee games. He called and told me to get ready as he was taking me to a game. I told him I was too busy. He incredulously inquired, "What the h—- are you so busy doing?" I replied, "Taking my pills."

GARBAGE: WHERE DOES IT ALL COME FROM?

Pascack Valley Community Life
August 21, 1996

"Where does all that garbage come from? Everyone has three or four barrels out in front of their house," my wife commented incredulously.

In my usual "Willy-the-know-all" fashion, I omnisciently explained. Society is overflowing with paper of every size, functional use and color.

In a big family, some years back, we all had napkins inserted in fancy napkin rings. "Keep them neat. They have to last for a week before they're washed," my mother would say. Today, our house of two (the kids are all gone) overflows with paper napkins and paper towels. We go through them like a thrashing machine goes through a corn field.

Nothing comes into the house "naked" anymore. Everything's wrapped in a carton, a box or durable paper. We all get a slew of daily and weekly newspapers and magazines. Who says TV has eradicated serious reading? And junk mail needs its own individual disposal barrel – there's so much of it.

Unfortunately, nobody has the traditional burn barrel in this day and age. We used to use it for everything we wanted to get rid of that we could put a match to. Along the way, some people even used to burn down the house!

Years ago, we also ate a good portion of our garbage. That is, we ate what currently constitutes garbage. We got rid of it via stews, hash, soups, etc. Today, leftovers often go out as garbage.

Recyclables is a whole new ball game. We recycle millions of cans and bottles. Thank goodness – or else we'd be buried in garbage!

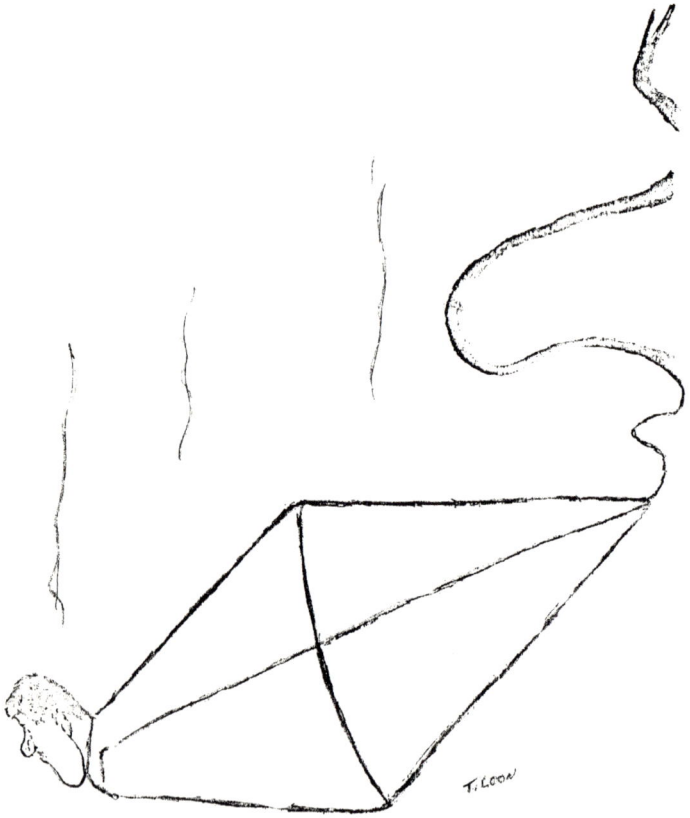

Clinton "Thunked", Then He Rose To Fly Again

PREPARE TO CRASH

The SandPaper
July 24, 1996

I don't totally dislike Clinton. I really don't. There are times when he soars majestically and then he's great. But he reminds me of the kites at Long Beach Island.

There's a wide prevalence of kite-flying here. Among the large number of beautiful, high-flying kites, there's always one that darts about crazily. It shoots up high, flits about in great style, then suddenly plunges downward. It catches itself and then climbs high again. Over and over again, it wildly plunges but seems to always gain control before crashing. It seems as if it will never crash. Then it dives earthward at breakneck speed and winds up with a "thunk", buried into the sand.

It's Clinton. Surely it is. If elected again, sooner or later, we are going to see the sudden "thunk". And when he's "thunking" we better be "thinking" about how we're going to get the nation back into even flight. Look at him go!

But hold your breath! You might even hide your eyes if it gets to you.

ALL IN THE FAMILY

The SandPaper
May 22, 1996

"If you kids don't knock it off, we're gonna lock up your mom and dad." The concept has a lot of sense in the arena of assessing responsibility and accountability. Others say it's unmitigated baloney. "Lock up the little darlings," they demand.

In Texas, judges can sentence the parents of juvenile offenders to community service. South Dakota judges can order parents to reimburse merchants if their children steal from them. California and Indiana hit at the pocketbooks. Parents can be held liable for the cost of housing the delinquent children in an institution. Jerk around with the law and parents can be the ones who see the inside of a jail.

Within the last few years, New Jersey and many other states have added new versions of parental responsibility laws to their juvenile criminal codes. Many parents have reservations about the laws but most agree that families just have to be held accountable.

All I can say is: Where were you when we needed you when we were engaged in organized crime investigations in the days of all those Page 2 newspaper stories about Murder Incorporated, "On the Waterfront", Crime Incorporated, Albert Anastasia, Carlo Gambino, Vito Genovese, "Mad Dog" Coll, etc.? We who worked in organized crime investigations had minimal success – until bugs and wiretaps were permitted under federal laws.

It would have been so simple. We could have said, "Albert, Carlo, Vito, we'll fix you for all the horrible things you are doing. We are going to lock up your mama or your papa, or both." That most likely would have solved the monumental problems. You know how tough most of the old-fashioned mothers and fathers were in those days. I can envision Albert, Carlo, Vito and the others begging, "Please don't tell my mother. I'll get in line, I'll get out of the rackets. I swear on my mother's grave."

Things could have been so much better, and we could have had a better case close-out record. I think, however, "Mickey the Wiseguy" would have been a lost cause.

READER APPRECIATES WOMEN

The Leader
May 16, 1996

All wives and mothers are counterparts to that invaluable employee who quietly performs so many functions and operations that it takes four or five employees to replace him or her upon their retirements.

Moms, those fantastic "gals" do the wash, prepare the meals, dress kids, tutor them, serve as a bus service, nurse the family (they seem to never get ill) and, these days, most of them perform full-time jobs out in the cruel business world. I only touched upon their diversity of demands to perform. My own wife does everything but lay brick, plumbing and electrical work. I marvel at how much they do.

My wife had to leave the house the other day to minister to an old high school schoolmate who was recovering from a major operation. She managed to fit in another accomplishment. She inquired, "You can get something to eat at noon – right?" My blasé response was, "No problem."

The phone rang, someone knocked on the front door, and I was in the midst of cooking – concurrently. Smoke began to fly from the frying pan, smoke alarms "blared out" and I was personally *alarmed*, fuming, embarrassed and at my wit's end. I was badly discharging a few operations normally done by my wife while she's in the midst of nine others.

Dole or Clinton could have stolen the march and grabbed a lot of votes by proposing that all wives and mothers are entitled to full Social Security benefits at the age of sixty – regardless of whether they have ever performed for even one day in the workplace. Workplace! I mean that other place away from their *routine* home duties. You don't think Congress will approve the Social Security deal? I'm sure, however, they'll go along with appropriating money for medals. But let's not shut down government over it. Realistically, however, the obstructionist party will lose the presidential election.

"I hate hot cereal!"

©1996 The Star-Ledger. All rights reserved. Reprinted with permission.

PUTTING A LID ON OUR IMPULSE TO HATE

The Star-Ledger
May 7, 1996

It's amazing what a wide range of people and things we profess to hate. We generally blurt out our feelings in moments of exasperation.

One of my young grandsons complains that he hates the high, hard fastball when hitting in baseball. "God," he says, "I can't hold off on it. I swing and I miss." My eldest daughter, when a little tyke, used to say, "I hate hot cereal with lumps in it." All my contemporaries say they loathe rap music. Actually, they mean they hate it.

My wife doesn't hate much in this world, but she gets highly indignant when young grandsons neglect to lift the toilet seat when going to the bathroom.

As for me, I hate… Stop! I mean I don't like… Stop! I'm rather averse to Bill and Hillary. There, I feel better already. My wife should really try harder to get used to the toilet seat.

THE IMPORTANCE OF GENES

Herald News
March 26, 1996

Genes are jiving around all over the ranch these days. They're on a lot of people's minds and seemingly, everyone's behavior patterns. They even cause some people to be sick. These people have bad genes for certain illnesses.

New Jersey's legislators have been kicking the genes around discussing how far we should go in denying insurance companies from using genetic test results in denying insurance coverage to potential victims of diseases such as cancer, sickle cell anemia and cystic fibrosis.

Even more captivating, however, was the identification of a gene tied not to disease but to personality traits. This novelty-seeking gene affects how impulsive, excitable, quick-tempered and extravagant we are. It's allegedly the first missing link between genes and personality. They claim that people who are above average in these genes are impulsive, fickle, excitable, quick-tempered and extravagant. Those scoring below average tend to be reflective, rigid, loyal, stoic, slow to anger and frugal. I can envision the guy being led to the electric chair crying out, "It's not that I claim I'm innocent – but my genes really did it."

It seems to me that genes are infinitely more important these days than designer jeans, and they don't cost a lot of money. You're stuck with what you got, and you surely do take them with you – for better or worse.

THEY'RE THE UNSUNG HEROES OF EDUCATION

Town News

February 21, 1996

One of the troubling current focuses of states and the nation is upon education. We must indeed evince concern for its cost, as we do in many other vital arenas, but the quality of the output, in the main, is excellent. It's much better than the critics claim it to be. We're not discussing inner-city problems. They're a thing apart.

The President, the Governor and the nation's current hero of the moment, in a reflective mode, often harkens back and recalls a "great 7th or 8th grade English, Math or Science teacher." The teacher was big in the individual's life. The one who reminisces was old enough, when in the 7th and 8th grades, to vividly recall the value of the teacher's affirmative contribution. The real unsung heroes of education, however, are those K to 3rd–4th grade teachers.

The little children are not very long away from the womb and are closely attached to the mother for virtually everything when they come to those teachers for their introduction to education. The detachment procedure must be adroitly and tenderly handled. These "surrogate mothers" must transitionally provide the love and warmth of the actual mothers. However, the restrictive concept of discipline and society's demands for rule/law adherence must be sidled into the learning process. Competitive sports, sportsmanship and the place of exercise and sports in one's daily life enter the menu of living. The ability to be assertive but also get along with others is taught. It's not easy. The fundamental need and value of learning and education are introduced to the little tykes. Respect for one's country and its values are presented to avid, anxious ears.

The now famous writer, Robert Fulghum, wrote a captivating book, titled, *All I Really Need To Know I Learned in Kindergarten*. Not quite accurate! He was a little too restrictive. He and all the other "hes and shes" learned it between K and 3rd–4th. And so, three cheers for those unique people who have that vital role in preparing our children for the joys, restrictions, games, learning ability, respect and all the other components which comprise life's game of living.

My wise son-in-law teaches at the 7th and 8th grade levels. For many years, neighbors have been telling me that he is the best damn Math teacher extant. He holds, however, that almost all K–4th grade teachers have minimal trouble in adapting to teaching higher grades. All teachers, conversely, can't teach at the K–3rd/4th levels. They're the "aces" who do not get the great respect they deserve.

WHERE ANGELS FEAR TO TREAD

Community Life
February 7, 1996

I was genuinely pleased, just recently, to have a man for whom I have unbounded respect, suggest that I am a good man – "almost saintly, from time to time."

I was taken aback – but I admit, rather puffed up and pleased. I modestly mentioned to him, however, that he was very generous in his praise. I suggested that I do try to be good and decent and possibly am sixty to seventy percent of the time. The other twenty per cent of the time, I'm very normal – fluctuatingly good, bad and indifferent. The other five percent of the time, I slip into the role of an unmitigated wretch – with a capital W. Some of my friends would contend the figures are reversed.

I reminded him that I'm just like all the other bipeds that are walking around on this earth. Few of us are capable of flapping the wings of angels. We'd flop to earth with a "plop", like the Wright brothers in their initial attempts at flight.

My wife thinks she's an angel but I reminded her that she better have B-29 wings for support. "Don't rely upon the wings of an angel," I tell her. She suggests that I shouldn't blow flames at her "wings" as she floats about when we go where we are both destined to go at some future date. Which says a lot for where she thinks I'm going.

WHAT IT TAKES TO BE AN AMERICAN INSTITUTION

Community Life
January 29, 1996

America abounds with institutions. Sort of like nouns, they can be a person, place or thing. It must be wonderful to be an institution.

We have Babe Ruth, Joe DiMaggio, Niagara Falls, Mary Poppins and the Statue of Liberty.

One can claim a little fame by being related to an institution.

The other day, someone mentioned an old actor, Reginald Owens. "Who's he?" someone else inquired.

"He was a famous character actor, and most particularly, he was the old retired sea captain who constantly discharged a cannon from the rooftop of the house where Mary Poppins (a major league institution) was residing."

Time flies and some people's fame vanishes with the passage of years.

Some institutions cease to be. I loved Ray Bolger and his "loose-as-a-goose" style of dancing.

Ray was regarded as an institution in the musical comedy arena. He's no longer easily remembered.

But mention the Scarecrow in the *Wizard of Oz* and you'll recall a lot of institutions. There were Judy Garland, the picture itself, and Ray Bolger – the Scarecrow.

The nation has had Bing Crosby, Shirley Temple, Frank Sinatra, Guy Lombardo's New Year's Eves, Hollywood Boulevard, Broadway and 42nd Street, the Grand Canyon and so many more.

The "old" Madison Square Garden... truly an institution. It had Dempsey, Tunney, the Rangers, the Americans (the first New York City hockey team), the Millrose games, the Knicks, the NIT tournament (when that was the epitome of basketball) Bill Tilden, the 6-Day bike races, Billy Graham and on and on.

My claim to fame – I ice speedskated at the Garden, the end-all of sports and major public events, in the days when few people managed to hit that jackpot.

The problem is, I'm the only one who remembers.

DOWNSIZING: WHO IS LEFT TO BUY?

Town News
January 17, 1996

We daily read that some famous business management hotshot has downsized one of America's biggest corporations. Costs are naturally down, profits are up, and "bond and stock holders will get increasing yield on their investments this year." Hurrah for the hotshots.

The firm is planning to drop forty, fifty, or sixty thousand employees during the coming year – but they intend to do it with tenderness and commiseration. It's capitalism in action, with a heart.

Capitalism is all tied in with private property, freedom of enterprise, freedom of exchange, and freedom of contract. Entrepreneurship is an integral part. It has its problems but heck, it's much better than any of the other failed economic systems we've seen throughout the world.

It's my own empirical concept, however, that all economic systems have as their ultimate and highly desirable objectives, the making available of goods and services to the people. Capitalism has assuredly done that better than all other economic systems.

These leadership boys are, however, giving me more than a little apprehension. Day by day, they're downsizing. Explicitly, they're "canning" a lot of employees. And these guys and girls (the canned ones) are what is known as the "market". They buy the goods and services. I just hope the hotshots stop in time. If one carries it to the ultimate, we shall have the most downsized, efficient business organizations conceivable with fantastic yields to the investors. But there will be nobody to buy the goods and services.

They will all have been downsized. They'll have no dough in their wallets.

With my little old singular degree in banking and finance, I guess I'm simplistic in my understanding of the modern economic doings. I worry.

NEXT ON MTV: SOCIETY UNPLUGGED

Town News

January 3, 1996

To the Editor,

Many of my friends become upset that they seem to be on the wrong side on so many national issues. Indeed, the vast majority of the nation's population, Democrats and Republicans alike are chagrined.

We're beleaguered by the battering we take in newspapers and on TV. I find myself sometimes joining with a large number of them who look upon this as a sort of loose-jointed conspiracy. Not so. When we stop, stand back and make a sensible analysis, it's surely no conspiracy. It's a "cultural disconnect". They deign to explain everything to us in their weird, confused and stilted intellectual condescension. Many of this divisive crew are highly educated, which is a sad commentary on advanced education.

Though they generally represent, at best, fifteen to twenty percent of the nation in its thinking, they sincerely but disconcertingly believe they represent the true thoughts and feelings of this period in history. And they are going to convince the rest of us, come hell or high water, despite the fact that every poll reflects their fundamental lack of understanding what America is all about. They remind me of the petulant woman who stamps her foot and exclaims, "I don't care whether all of you feel that way – I'm right." She's adamantly resolute, though she is one of twelve. When not dominating conversations, she's writing editorials.

T C

NEW YORK CITY AND DIO–3ND IN WWII

Naval Intelligence Professionals Quarterly
Winter 1995

New York City was an exciting place to be during the early stages of World War II. If one was assigned to the Third Naval District Naval Intelligence Office, it was a truly fascinating place to report for duty each morning. Dynamic cases rapidly unfolded.

I was personally funneled to the DIO–3ND for possible acceptance as a yeoman. I still had a term to go (nights) before I obtained my degree, thus precluding my applying to come on board as an ensign rather than a yeoman. I completed the "folding wonder" application and sat back for several months before the extensive background investigation was completed. Happily, I was accepted.

When I reported for duty, the office was already deep in the investigation of the *Normandie* sinking (a French passenger liner confiscated by the US Government. ed.). The office abounded with famous names. Many were top people in industry who served as administrators or vital cogs in Strategic Intelligence. It was a revelation for me to see Vincent Astor, Jock Whitney and men of that stature holed up in relatively small offices hard at work. They were invaluable for their contacts in relation to high-level information gathering.

A nucleus of outstanding men in the criminal investigative field were recruited. Herman McCarthy came directly from the legendary District Attorney Frank Hogan's office, where he successfully prosecuted Fritz Kuhn, the German Bund leader. Another personality, John Cye Cheasty, became nationally known as a Treasury Department Intelligence Unit Special Agent before the war. He and a partner broke the notorious politics/vice empire in

South New Jersey headed by "Nockey" Johnson. He did it through the perceptive, but earthy, approach of linking Mr. Johnson to income from brothels – and estimating income by counting the sheets or towels at the various houses of prostitution. It was ingenious, good criminal investigation and a blow to long-festering wrongdoing.

My dear friend, Robert Morris, was already hard at work in charge of the DIO–3ND Communist Section when I arrived there. Bob was a brilliant young lawyer who started his career as an attorney with the Rapp-Coudert Committee, which had probed Communist infiltration into the New York City Public School system. He came to the DIO armed with unique background and experience. Though America was an ally of the Soviets at this point, the intelligence community was mindful that the Soviets would in all probability be our enemy in the future. The DIO wisely devoted some resources to this problem as an ancillary operation in the midst of the main thrusts – Nazism, Fascism and Japanese espionage. During a subsequent phase of the war, Bob served as Officer in Charge of the Advance Section of Psychological Warfare on Guam for Admiral Nimitz's headquarters. After the war, Bob was acclaimed for his role as Chief Counsel to the US Senate Internal Security Committee.

I alluded to the "Lucky" Luciano case of WWII in a previous commentary in the *NIP Quarterly*. Parenthetically, it should be noted that the office of former Prosecutor Tom Dewey (then Governor of New York) furnished DIO–3ND a batch of talent, which had previously participated in the racket-busting in the New York City area. One of their most famous cases was the Murder Incorporated investigation. This talented group of investigators became a part of the B–3 Section of DIO–3ND under Cdr. Harold Haffenden and Lt. Maurice Kelly.

Another Section, B–5, was a large and vital part of DIO–3ND because it operated in conjunction with the world's largest and busiest port – New York Harbor. Its pace was accelerated because of the destructiveness of the Atlantic Ocean submarine warfare. We worked closely with the War Shipping Administration. This vital B–5 operation was later turned over to the US Coast Guard. B–10 (intelligence pertaining to our industrial complex) was understandably large. The whole metropolitan New York City area was replete with large industries tied in with the war economy.

There was always something new and explosive tumbling upon the scene. A surprise telephone call that a "midget submarine" had landed out at the tip of Long Island seemed bizarre. It was very real, however, and ONI agents handled the initial frantic-pace phases of the investigation because the call had come to the DIO–3ND Duty Watch. The FBI then came on board and handled the wrap-up phases of the case to its successful conclusion. Germany's venture into this novel form of submarine utilization was frustrated from the outset.

There are many other stories, of course, but with the restrictions upon intelligence operations since the days of the Church Committee, it's not popular, or wise, to discuss details of certain intelligence operations – even long completed operations. Many would be totally unacceptable these days. The DIO–3ND's famous Surreptitious Entry cases are a prime example. However, one could dig up the *Reader's Digest* 1964 edition of *Secrets and Spies* to read a digest of the Willis George book *Surreptitious Entry*. He described the exciting, midnight entries into various locations in the New York City area – some of them into foreign government offices. The operations were highly productive. Willis, however, was talking when he should have been listening when he wrote his book. Much of the information he discussed was still highly classified at that time.

The DIO–3ND WWII office was never dull. I merely touched upon a minuscule part of its operations. Even the nightlife was fantastic in those lively days of the Stork Club, the 21 Club, Leon and Eddie's, the Copacabana, the Latin Quarter and countless others. I hung out at the Bossert Roof in Brooklyn – yes, Brooklyn! The view from the Bossert Roof, looking over at the New York City skyline, far exceeded the view from the famous Rainbow Room in the Rockefeller Center – looking over at Brooklyn.

As mentioned earlier, there was an incredible diversity of personalities working at the DIO, ranging from an Astor, a Whitney and a Vanderbilt down to ordinary but intelligent and carefully selected middle-class kids. My buddies were Al Kloeblin, Sid Smith and "Mr. New York Athletic Club" Eddie Moclair, one of

New York's colorful and famous citizens. Cdr. Rudy Caputo worked there, then went to China with Admiral Miles and his famous "Rice Paddy Sailors" and came back to the dio to work as a Special Agent after the war. He was my boss and my pal at the DIO, where I also later worked as a Special Agent.

Jim Murray, Paul Alfieri, Joe Kaitz and Tony Marsloe were members of the group that handled the Luciano case. They flew to Italy and followed up on the leads furnished by the mob. Working with contacts there, they contributed immeasurably to the campaign in Italy. Paul Alfieri was highly decorated. He virtually accepted the surrender of the Italian Fleet as it fled the Germans and turned itself over to the Allies. I believe Ben Brucia and Joe Titolo (members of the post-war Intelligence Reserve) were also in this operation.

Jim Murray became a New Jersey State Senator after the war. Paul Alfieri served with Caputo and me as Special Agents in DIO–3ND, and later was Asst. Chief Investigator of the very productive New York State Crime Commission, Chief Investigator of the New Jersey Law Enforcement Council, and Director of Investigations of the Waterfront Commission of New York Harbor. Joe Kaitz was an old associate of Tom Dewey and was Governor Rockefeller's point man on law enforcement matters. On behalf of the Governor, he handled the structuring of the first mandatory police training law (for recruits) for the State of New York. This law then served as the model for all other states of the nation as they proceeded to enact their own laws. Joe was ultimately the New York Commissioner with the bi-state Waterfront Commission of New York Harbor. Tony Marsloe is a Captain in the Naval Reserve (and a longtime member of NIP. ed.). He was a Liquor Commissioner in New York State (along with Kaitz) and later became President of a liquor company.

I must reaffirm that we had diversity. Jim Gregory used to entertain us with attempts at acting. He later succeeded and played the lovable Inspector, over a period of many years, in the hit TV series *Barney Miller*. Many of the WWII DIO–3ND officers and enlisted men became outstanding leaders in government and industry in the post-war years.

RIGHT FOODS CURE MEDICAL PROBLEMS

The Leader

September 21, 1995

Dear Editor,

The right foods will *right* a lot of medical problems. You're worried about arteriosclerosis? Cut down on saturated fat and high-cholesterol chow. You're afraid cancer will do you in? Focus on monounsaturated fats, stay out of the sun, eat fiber-rich foods loaded with vitamins A and C, drink skim milk and go easy on the booze. High blood pressure's a concern? Throw away the salt shaker. You can guard against colds via chicken soup, chili peppers and – don't forget the fruits.

Let's face it. Fruits and vegetables are good for whatever ails you. You are not talking about "big-stuff" in the arena of ailments but you claim to be bedeviled by constipation? Reach out for high fiber foods, lots of water – and the old reliable fruits. You'll feel better and your disposition will materially improve.

You complain that your problem is that Clinton upsets you so much that he makes you ill? You are not alone. Look at what happened to Starr and friends. You better adhere to all the best food combinations, for now. In 2000, have a good, well-balanced breakfast and then go to the polls on election day and pull the right lever for President. We've got to keep everyone healthy – the nation, as a whole, included.

Sincerely,

T

IS THERE A LOT OF HOLLERING IN THE WHITE HOUSE?

Community Life
August 9, 1995

I'm deeply disturbed by screaming and angry tumult. I'm ashamed to admit, nevertheless, that I'm sometimes a five-star "tumulter" myself. I don't mean to be. I hate it, but too frequently I fall into the trap.

My father was an intimidating, almost frighteningly powerful man when he raised his voice and demanded order and obedience among his eight offspring. I resolved I'd never be like him.

But, I was young and in later life, my older brother-in-law commented to me, "Tom, with eight exuberant kids kicking around, the father has to be vigorous if he aspires to maintain order. It's essential to achieving tranquility around the household. Your Pop often blasted you guys – and winked in my direction. He was carrying out his fatherly mission."

I'm usually the model of conviviality, calmness and gentleness, but I "blow my top" more than I'd like to admit. I have a daughter in whose domicile a little loud debate sometimes takes place. I ask my grandsons, "You want to hang around here, amidst some hollering, or do you want to go home to your own roosting place where there's another vintage of hollering?" I figure I should give the little guys a choice as to which bedlam suits their desire.

I've read in the *Spectator* that Hillary Clinton is a veritable hell-on-wheels around the "happy home". But that's a conservative magazine. However, the *National Review*, another conservative magazine, holds the same view. Recently, several liberal magazines sheepishly admitted the same.

There must be substance. Imagine how much hollering and

screaming there must be in the happy home – the White House home, that is. We holler at the kids for leaving some messes around. Make a mess, clean it up, I say. With the White House being a total mess these days, the tumult must be unbearable.

W C Fields used to level people complaining about things by the laconic inquiry, "Would you rather be in Philadelphia?" Henceforth, I'll level the kids by inquiring, "Hey Jesse, T J and Jarrett, knock off the mischief and clean up the mess." If they grumble, I'll ask them, "Would you rather be in the White House?"

EXCUSE ME?

The Post Review
July 16, 1995

America lives via new usage of words. Generally, but not always, euphemism is the name of the game.

The in-guys and gals use them to the ultimate. It's a tangential part of political correctness. They "firm up" things. I guess they go up on the second deck to do all this firming.

They're always interested in the "bottom line". I don't think any of them read the story in between. There are a lot of marvelous stories out there. They're constantly in search of "problem solvers". I wonder what the hell they think my mother did with all those eight kids.

If you're on the move upwards, however, you have to parrot the in-words. I never did. I never got a "collar". I arrested the bloke. I never got information from a "snitch". I got it from an informant, or a source of information.

Attorney General Janet Reno recently tossed a new slice of baloney into the euphemism cutter. Janet declared that she was curious about the circumstances under which Commerce Secretary Brown came up with about a half million smackeroos by selling his interest in a company "firmed up" with Washington businesswoman Nolanda Hill. He never put a thin dime into the venture. Ms. Reno wondered if there had been any "linkage" between the payment to Brown and his official position. She continued to wonder long enough to ask for a Special Prosecutor to smell around a little to determine whether something was a little rotten.

I had a dear friend, a number of years ago, who went "up the river" for a short period of term. He said he was engaged in collecting political campaign funds. The jury said it was a slight case of shakedown or kickback. While in criminal investigations, we were always checking on the Anastasias, Sottos, Catenas, Gambinos and sundry gentlemen of dubious character. We often made "kickback cases".

Fortunately, Janet Reno came along too late for a lot of the boys. They could have adduced the euphemistic defense of, "Sir, we were not seeking any illegal, immoral or questionable shakedowns or kickbacks that would inure to the detriment of society. We were merely flirting around with a little linkage." That's linkage – like in sausage or baloney.

COLLEGE GRAD BLUNDERS

The Record
July 12, 1995

To the Editor,

Back in 1943, I completed my work for a degree at New York University, but could not make the graduation because my Navy duties precluded my attending. However, NYU recently invited us old grads to don a cap and gown and take part in this year's ceremonies.

Neil Diamond was an honored guest at this year's graduation, which was televised. He sang. He talked. One young graduate, in cap and gown, excitedly told the world how much she enjoyed it but wished "he had sang more".

I contend that someone who graduates from college should recognize a past participle in broad daylight and know she should have said "had sung". With a degree, one hopes the learned individual will not blurt out on television, "We was all happy," "Me and him graduated" – or "I wish he had sang."

Petty? Possibly. But it's also an embarrassing commentary upon the quality of recipients of degrees, particularly from my own alma mater. We don't all talk that way. It's enough to impel one to consider turning in his sheepskin if the quality of grammar doesn't improve.

T C

CUT THE CRUDENESS

The Leader
June 1, 1995

I'm old fashioned. I love the moonlight and I love old-fashioned songs. But I sure didn't lead a sheltered life.

I served in the Navy during World War II and I kicked around in politics. The men in the Navy and, more particularly, along the legendary, turbulent New York–New Jersey waterfront, were really tough guys. There was no acting here. They could utilize a curse word – with adaptation – as a noun, verb, adjective or adverb. I lived with the rough life and sometimes, adaptively, used the prevailing "vocabulary" in interrogations – but I left it at the doorstep when I came home at night. I would not dream of exposing my wife and children to this linguistic plague.

Young children, today, hear it everywhere (including at home) and they'd make a hardened longshoreman blush with their own objectionable utilization. Washington, Jefferson, Franklin and Lincoln would be bewildered and aghast if they were miraculously invited as guests to an Oprah, Sally, Donahue or an evening entertainment show. Hollywood has no sense of shame. It seems nobody has.

What amuses me, however, is the pretension to toughness by this generation. Would that they could be transplanted to the old waterfront. They'd meet people talking tough who were the real thing. These modern pretenders, conversely, are a ridiculous, mimicking bunch with no reason for their grossness. They not only sound crude, they sound silly. They are silly to not aspire higher. A good vocabulary would serve them well.

THERE'S NO SECRET KEY AROUND

The Post Review
March 30, 1995

A young mathematician from California has created a powerful new code that will prevent hackers from snooping through private computer files. The code, called "Snuffle", would make text appear to be utter gibberish to anyone who didn't have a secret key to decrypt it. It would be like breaking the Japanese code during WWII.

The Snuffle code is based on an algorithm, a step-by-step recipe that turns raw ingredients – readable text, for example – into gobbledygook by mixing it in a blender. To decode the gobbledygook, the trick is to build a Mixmaster with a reverse button that will put it back to the original ingredient.

So what's so great about the young genius' invention? I just completed my Income Tax return and the guys who wrote the instructions have been writing gobbledygook for years and years. President Clinton spoke for a couple of hours in his recent State of the Nation address and it was unadulterated gobbledygook to the nation. Lawyers have been speaking gobbledygook for years (the O J Simpson case is a prime example). Try to get a youth a college scholarship and you'll meet up with you know what. Politicians, in general, run whole campaigns predicted on gobbledygook.

Heck, I don't think this young man came up with a new version of the wheel or the equivalent of the cotton gin. Any of us who have been kicking around on this earth for any degree of time at all have long lived with gobbledygook. Nobody ever gives us the secret key. We're so used to it, we don't even ask if there is a key floating around.

Indeed, society rather tacitly appreciates that we must not make easy the comprehension of the gobbledygook. The young inventor got a shock. He could not market his new and wondrous code. He was prevented from doing so under a law designed to "protect national security cryptographic tools". He will now have to attempt to "decipher" this new problem.

INMATES SHOULD ANTE UP

Commercial Leader
February 23, 1995

Dear Editor,

In life, one does not have to invent the telephone, the computer or the cotton gin to attain his place in history. More often, it's enough to build that "better mousetrap".

It may be that Jack Terhune, the sheriff of Bergen County, has come up with his contribution to the better mousetrap hall of fame. He announced that county inmates residing in the Bergen County Jail in Hackensack will henceforth be charged co-payments for many medical services. Starting January 2, the county commenced a $10 fee for most doctor and dental visits and $2 as a prescription handling fee. It will yield the income to the county coffers. It will also discourage frivolous calls for doctors which are motivated by a desire to break the boredom of a day in the life of a resident of the county jail.

When one appreciates that it costs $20,000 for a year of domiciling a prisoner, it becomes apparent that cost cutting has to be achieved. I have dear friends who are employed by county and state government and they don't do as well as the guys housed in our county bastille. Jack Terhune is reaching out to cut costs that are not mandated by the state. He has no control over mandated items. In short, he's reining in on anything that's reinable.

I'm told that the governmental legal eagles were dubious whether the sheriff could charge the prisoners. Terhune's contention was, however, that the courts said medical treatment *must* be provided – but they didn't say who had to pay for it. Why not encourage the boys in the jug to be good citizens and chip in their proper share like thee and me? Makes sense to me.

As a matter of fact, I think we should see just how far we can carry this good thing while we're on a roll and before some mischievous judge tries to establish his claim to omniscience by upsetting the apple cart.

Heck, all those Wall Street maneuverers and John Gotti and friends have to pay rent wherever they are residing at the moment. Why not tell them they've got to ante up for room and board if they insist on committing unsocial acts and wind up behind bars? What's so illogical about that? There may be no end to this taxpayer bonanza that Jack Terhune has kicked off. How about the "rags" the prisoners wear? We could set up a little K-Mart in the joint and really get into the merchandising arena.

Nevertheless, I think Jack Terhune has opened up all kinds of opportunities for economical good government. He should continue to ignore the opinions of the legal boys as to whether we can do this or that. Just do it. It's easy to go along with the fait accompli.

Interestingly, Gov. George Pataki of New York has said he'd like to explore the concept that Terhune is using in Bergen County. And we are all mindful that imitation is the sincerest form of flattery. I think we should all agree that it will be a great day when every prisoner, upon entering his new home, is asked: "What will it be while you are with us, cash, VISA or MasterCard?"

Sincerely,

T

IS IT LIKE "SPRING BREAK"?

Town News
January 25, 1995

President and Mrs. Clinton spent their New Year's weekend at Hilton Head Island, SC where they took part in Renaissance Weekend, "an annual family retreat for leaders in politics, business, science, law and the arts."

The news report described them as "leaders" – I didn't. I guess they so described themselves in their press release. That's how leaders are often created.

I read in another press release that many of the participants were volunteers in Clinton's run for the presidency. A goodly number of others had official roles in his presidential campaign. Some have been active in stirring the devil's brew that has recently been passed off as the nation's domestic and foreign policy.

I hope none of them are doing their Renaissancing around in my neighborhood. I'd like to know who these Peter Pans are. I might inadvertently go to one for advice on my financial portfolio, legal matters or the desirability of purchasing a Monet, Rubens or Renoir.

In the science arena, I'm okay. I rigidly stick to my two fifteen-year-old grandsons as my advisers. They never cease to amaze me and thankfully, they never went to Renaissance Weekend. They assured me they never went. They weren't even quite sure what it is. One wondered if it's something like "spring break" at Fort Lauderdale. I admitted I was not quite sure myself but I guessed it's not as much fun.

IS SUPERHIGHWAY REALLY A MIRACLE?

Town News

January 18, 1995

We constantly read and hear about the miracles of fax and the Information Superhighway. We've long lived with radio and TV. Everybody's raving about our progress. People are rolling out of bed and going to work, at home, in their work clothes – their pajamas. Frankly, I think that the communications revolution is the worst darn thing that ever hit America.

It used to be that one got up in the morning, pulled on his shoes and thought to himself, "I've gotta get a new pair of shoelaces. I can't continue with that knot even though it's unobtrusively placed." That was a big problem.

The retiree rather tranquilly went about puttering around in the backyard. The teacher went to work and taught, and the plasterer went to his job and floated plaster on the walls.

Everyone did his thing. It was a calm, relatively untroubled atmosphere. We didn't know so much, so quickly about everybody and everything.

With these miraculous forms of communication, we know all the problems of the county, state, nation and world – immediately. We know the trials and tribulations of every last sufferer in the world. It's tension laden. It's causing ulcers, diverticulitis and heart problems. I've already had diverticulitis and heart problems. I don't know who to sue, CNN, the radio industry, the inventor of fax or the TV industry.

Oh for the good old days of smoke signals, semaphore and even telegraph communications. Life was good. We didn't know as much – all at once. It's tolerable to learn about one horrible event at a time. Worrying about forgetting to put the garbage out used to be a big thing. Compare that with the news that a terrorist group might blow up Peekskill, Guttenberg or Dumont.

An ulcer is in the making. Come to think about it, the Pony Express was a great means of communicating. With the normal dosage of one crisis at a time, people were given recuperative time in between. Just don't tell me all the world's problems while I make way with one small breakfast. It's hard enough to digest my breakfast and "my own" problems each morning. The world's problems, on top, is too much for me to handle.

HEY, WATCH YOUR LANGUAGE!

The Record

December 12, 1994

I've found that life is a never-ending series of fulcrum relationships. There's good and evil; rights and duties; euphoric happiness and abysmal depression; win and lose – and on and on.

Youth sports is another prime example of the fulcrum principle. They afford an opportunity for one to learn and participate in the sport or sports of one's desire.

Young parents generously contribute their time towards instructing other peoples' kids. It's a truly noble enterprise. A bustling, gregarious, happy atmosphere at the games affords entertainment to young and old. This is the beneficent, uplifting flip side to the whole shebang.

A dubious side is insidiously creeping in. Did I forget the adjective "ugly"?

Youth sports in recent years has become an "icon" of sorts. It's been in the realm of God, country, apple pie and one's mother-in-law. One dare not criticize.

It reminds me of the old days with boards of education. If one even wondered about an item in the budget at a board meeting, an arm came out from the blue and stamped "Neanderthal" on the miscreant's forehead with indelible ink for the whole community to behold.

Now we are reading about a disconcerting aspect of youth sports. Win at any cost, five days a week of practice, games and practices in the rain, cursing the umpires, fisticuffs, and various unseemly behavior are creeping into what was once a happy, idealistic atmosphere.

There are disputes over the turf – football vs soccer. Who gets the largest share of the recreation pie of funds is a contentious consideration.

Some of the fathers want the little kids to be everything as athletes that they themselves were not. It's becoming a thing of "parents' recreation" more than it is "youth recreation".

We're learning that some coaches even curse the kids, when in a losing endeavor.

One of our municipalities, Woodcliff Lake, is on the brink of enacting an ordinance making "severe unsportsmanlike conduct" by spectators a petty disorderly person's offense. A state senator is pushing for a law that would make it a felony to assault a referee or umpire. A limitation on practice sessions is relevant.

If it's as bad as we're hearing, I better bone up on my defensive tactics that we taught up at the Police Academy while I was director.

I frequently watch the grandchildren taking part in sports. I'll also have to watch my language for I've fallen into the trap of some pretty powerful language since retiring from the Waterfront Commission and the Police Academy.

With daughters no longer in the house, I'm getting a little careless. I don't care what kind of language a lot of these ten-year-olds are using as they pass the house on the way to school. I'm going to mend my ways.

I sure hope that the minority of egregious parents will do the same.

OBSERVATIONS ON AGING – THE GREAT EQUALIZER

Community Life
September 14, 1994

One of life's great equalizers is old age. The potbellies at the local pool look the same on the retired corporate vice-presidents as they do on the retired clerk. One's place in the American Experience Mortality tables qualifies one for membership in some exclusive clubs. In addition to receiving Social Security checks, the individual has the enjoyment of membership in the American Association of Retired Persons (AARP) and all its derivative benefits.

The senior citizen is usually retired and the pension is the primary determinant of one's lifestyle.

When I was a big "crime buster" with the Waterfront Commission of New York Harbor, I was a "big guy" in the eyes of everyone on the piers (longshoremen, pier superintendents, steamship officials, etc.). However, in retirement, the ILA longshoremen get better pensions and health insurance benefits than I do. It's a good thing I believed in the old Benjamin Franklin maxims and saved some money. Although when we go on senior citizen bus trips, we all travel together equalized in every respect.

In old age, deficiencies are often charitably overlooked. When the commentary is made by an offended neighbor, "He makes the stupidest remarks," or "He told a crude 'off-color' story," someone will inevitably defend the miscreant. "He's old and doesn't know what he's saying," will often be the response.

They "label us" all in the same "package". It's all a part of the accommodating posture that society applies to people they presume are drifting into decreased mental capacity.

I've noticed that many retired people have a broad spectrum of views on everything – politics, the right or wrong of attacking the Chicapoo Indian tribe, abortion, the superiority of old-time athletes over the present, and everything old and new under the sun. Young people often agree, under the syndrome I've already described. It's not nice, however, when they surreptitiously wink at each other.

I personally think the waves of opinion that emanate from oldsters are partially tied to a new-found freedom – they no longer have to "kowtow" to bosses. The world's great sycophants are set free. Like their bosses of yore, they're free to spout inane and ridiculous platitudes without contradiction. And all along the route, people are prone to say, "Don't get mad at him, he's an old man."

Unfortunately, there's sometimes an irreverent one in the midst who spoils the fun with the rejoinder, "The old fool doesn't know what he's talking about – and he deserves a good swift boot in the buttocks."

Wait until he gets old and thinks he, too, is omniscient.

ON BEING MARRIED TO A CANDIDATE

The Beachcomber
July 2, 1994

To the Editor,

The young lady being pursued by a beau is in a situation frighteningly identical to that of the candidate seeking the presidency. A monumentally serious problem is endemic to both. The young lady should try to appreciate that she is fundamentally only *infatuated*. She should get to know the beau in depth before marriage, for she is venturing into long-lasting, serious business.

The electorate must also look beyond quick attraction to the candidate and etch deeply in their own minds the wise words of Tennyson. The young maiden and the electorate are in the same boat. Tennyson said:

> As the husband is, the wife is
> Thou art mated to a clown
> And the grossness of his nature
> Will have the weight to drag thee down

The young lady who hopes her love will change the qualities of the less-than-desirable suitor is inevitably doomed to failure and disappointment. The electorate who *marries* the wrong candidate without sufficient knowledge of his background is also in for a failed marriage. The young bride can tell the clod to pack his bags and go. The failure with a candidate, however, is catastrophic for the nation.

T C

A FAT LIP?

The Post Review
January 20, 1994

Dear Editor,

I have a serious complaint against many top vocalists concerning their rendition of *The Star Spangled Banner* and many famous musical "chestnuts" written by some of our well-known song writers.

They interject weird, discordant, cacophonous tremolos that distort the melody to a degree that one wonders what in God's name they're singing. "That's the National Anthem? That's *Silent Night*? You could fool me. Indeed you did."

If I were the composer, I'd reach out to Houdini to temporarily deliver me from the grave so that I might fly quickly to the stage and deliver a right cross to the "mush" of the grievous offender. A fat lip might get the alleged vocalist back on the melodious track.

Sincerely,

T

GRANDPA TRIES TO ANSWER QUERY

Suburbanite

December 8, 1993

I truly enjoy being a grandfather and take pleasure in sagaciously answering the many probative inquiries directed to me by fertile young minds.

Last week, one alert grandson asked me what the acronym NOW stands for. I drew one of those blanks one sometimes encounters at the age of seventy-five and said I knew the W stood for women. I told him I thought the N stood for nutsy.

I shall have to get back to him with the correction but I think the quick recollection was not too far off the mark.

THE BIRDS KNOW REAL MUSIC

Pascack Valley Community Life
June 17, 1993

My contemporaries and I were born during a tough age. We lived during the Depression; we paid our way through college at night; we fought in World War II; and then we got hit with a "notch" when we collected our Social Security checks. But the Almighty has a way of balancing things. He gave us good music in our time.

I feel sorry for our youths, who got stuck with hard rock and rap and other forms of cacophony. They don't know what the sound of beautiful, entertaining music is – unless their parents have strapped them to a chair and made them sit through obligatory sessions of WPAT, WHUD or a good collection of old records. Much of our music had a touch of poetry with lyricists such as Lorenz Hart, Oscar Hammerstein, Ira Gershwin, Cole Porter and countless more.

The big bands gave us a feast of beautiful sound that, in its own province of music, rivaled Tchaikovsky, Brahms, Verdi, Victor Herbert, Mozart and Puccini. You could sit up late at night and listen to the great bands on the four big radio stations, WABC, WJZ, WEAF and WOR. From 11 P.M. on into the morning, each station had a different band, every fifteen minutes, until the stations shut down for the night.

There would be Freddie Martin from the Coconut Grove in California, Johnny Messner from the McAlpin Grill Room in New York City, Charley Spivak from the Edgewater Beach Hotel in Chicago and Henry King from the Palmer House in Chicago. Then there was a new batch – Frankie Carle, Russ Morgan, Isham Jones, Glenn Miller, Jimmy Dorsey, Ray Noble and on and on. There were literally hundreds of wonderful top-flight big name bands appearing throughout the nation at hotels, nightclubs and dance halls. And we danced a lot in those days.

Vocalists were superb – Sinatra, Eberly, Como, Doris Day, Helen Forrest, Nat King Cole were just a few. Indicative of how good they were during the days of our "real music", they are still playing the old bands and vocalists, over and over again, on radio stations.

It's interesting to observe that the birds sang beautifully sixty years ago when I was a youth spending our summer away from Hudson County in the "country" in River Edge.

I've lived many years in Bergen County in later life and the birds still sing the same as they always did, with no perverting interjection of hard rock or rap. They innately know what real music is. They're smarter than our current breed of music purveyors who are busting our eardrums with discordant sound purporting to be music. The birds know better.

LIFE IS LIKE A BUTCHER'S SCALE

Pascack Valley Community Life
May 26, 1993

One of the classic magazine covers of all times was done by the legendary Norman Rockwell. He depicted a conniving butcher discreetly asserting pressure with his finger pushing the weighing scale downward – and a sharp-looking, contriving old lady slyly pushing a finger upward on the opposite side of the scale. Each is astounded at the result. Each was attempting to cheat the system.

We must remember that, under normal circumstances, life is a veritable butcher's scale. If untampered with by people who want to give themselves a wrongful "edge", it works beautifully.

Deliver me from people who are forever endeavoring to tilt the scales – much like the unscrupulous butcher and the cheating old lady in the famous Rockwell magazine cover.

Too many people in life use crib sheets when taking tests; offer or solicit kickbacks for jobs and contracts; push and shove in lines instead of waiting their individual turn; and in general, foul up the fair implementation of the system.

Dangerous cutting in and out on the New Jersey Turnpike and the Garden State Parkway is a form of tilting the scale towards one's own rapid progress to the jeopardy of others.

Fraudulent, baseless suits pervert the legal system and unjustly enrich the suers. Finagling with the social programs such as unemployment insurance, workers' compensation, Social Security and welfare puts dollars in one's pockets and takes them out of society's pockets.

There are many arenas in which improper hands are being exerted on the butcher's scale of daily life.

It sometimes seems as if everyone in the whole world is frantically endeavoring to nudge the scale up or down to one's own advantage.

Be calm, however, as my late, sagacious brother-in-law once commented, "Tom, there're a lot of clam cakes out there in the world. The redeeming factor, nevertheless, is that there are more good people out there than there are clam cakes."

IMPORTANT PROBLEMS

Sunday Post
May 16, 1993

"Vinnie, the Wise Guy", will undoubtedly escape arrest in the not too distant future for selling condoms to first graders, peddling marijuana in the grammar school hallways and making book on the outcome of the fourth grade baseball game. They're all on the threshold of legalization.

We can then get back to good old traditional problems of public schools, such as running in the halls, dress code violations, littering, throwing spitballs, chewing gum and talking out of turn in the classroom.

Isn't it delovely? We'll just keep working to legalize all those pesky youth problems like drug and alcohol abuse, pregnancy, rape and robbery.

The more we legalize and condone, the less we'll be distracted from handling the spitball throwers. Proper and purposeful perspective is the would-be name of the game. Hold one's breath and maybe legalization will lead to dulcet, blissful tranquility. "Vinnie the Wise Guy" could tell you that maybe it won't work. Dealing with probabilities is a part of his occupation.

However, many youths don't appreciate the seriousness of our old traditional problems like throwing spitballs and chewing gum. They've been distracted by the new breed of problems. But we elders are working hard to be rid of them. Hold your breath and hold your hats, children, we're in there pitching for you.

SPECIALIZATION – OH MY ACHING TOOTH

Pascack Valley Community Life
May 5, 1993

America grew economically great and robust through its application of scientific principles of management in the conduct of business. Fundamental principles were developed through years of practical experience. One of the essential principles which contributed to the economic greatness of America was specialization.

The principle of specialization rests upon the underlying concept that few men can do many things and do them well but most men can do a few things well if the scope of their activities is small enough. Charley Chaplin, in the moving picture, *Modern Times*, portrayed the poor guy who nearly went "nuts" in discharging his specialized responsibility on the assembly line.

One of the areas in which I think this nation went wrong, however, was taking away the tooth-pulling operation from the barber. Besides trimming hair he used to be the guy who pulled teeth, too.

I recently had an abscess. My dentist said he was averse to handling it. He sent me to a periodontist who took care of the infection. He sent me back to my dentist for a crown job. Shortly after the crowning, I had problems with my gums. My dentist then sent me to an endodontist for a root canal.

About a month later, I encountered the same gum problem. Not to my surprise, the endodontist told me I had a gum problem that was in no way related to the crown work or the root canal procedure. I was referred back to the same periodontist I had visited not too long ago. I was also out about $1,400 and back at square one.

We were better off when "Joe the barber" gave us our haircuts and, as an ancillary operation, pulled teeth. And he was much cheaper; he was not a high-priced specialist.

Sometimes change is not necessarily progress. Specialization is not always the best route to follow.

Oh, for the good old days of "Joe the barber" when he could give you a haircut and pull your tooth on the same visit! If he owned the shop, you weren't even expected to give him a tip. In some shops you could get your shoes shined while waiting for the barber – and it was not unusual to be able to bet on a number or a horse. "Joe" was a real old-fashioned "generalist".

MONDAY MORNING
QUARTERBACKING

Sunday Post
February 14, 1993

History reports upon Calvin Coolidge's lukewarm reception to having been chosen to run for vice-president of the nation. When the Republican convention telephoned "Cal" in Boston with the news, he turned to his wife and laconically said, "Nominated for Vice-President." She commented, "You're not going to take it, are you?" He responded, "I suppose I'll have to."

Mr. Coolidge wound up as our thirtieth president. He presided over a period in history known as the "Roaring Twenties" when business was booming and everyone was happy to "keep cool with Coolidge". We survived the Jazz Age and Prohibition.

During the first Clinton election, all the Democratic heavy hitters flirted with the thought of running for President but demurred. Even Al Gore, who was eventually elected Vice-President, initially coveted the Presidency. President Bush had those overwhelmingly favorable ratings after the Gulf War. He frightened away all the major competition. How do you take on someone with an eighty-five to ninety percent favorable rating?

I can envision the Clinton household around that time. Hillary most likely commented, "Nobody wants that nomination for President; you're not going to take it, are you?" Bill responded, "Nobody else will take it. I suppose I'll have to." At this moment in history, how would you like to be Mrs. Nunn, Mrs. Cuomo, Mrs. Gephardt, Mrs. Bradley, or a few others whose husbands were included among the leading contenders for the Democratic nomination? I can envision the good wife of some one of them, glaring over the dinner table at her beloved spouse and growling,

"Why couldn't you have been the one who supposed you had to take it? I'd be the First Lady today. I'd be plotting how I would change all those dishes, drapes and a multiplicity of other things women like to mess with. Damn, damn, damn, if only you had supposed correctly."

NO TIME FOR A FULL-TIME JOB

Community Life
January 13, 1993

Gee, am I not glad I'm retired? I don't know how I'd get everything done and make it through the day if I were not so.

I've resolved to take good care of my teeth – what's left of them – and minister to every single one of them, brushing well with ninety percent angle strokes.

The cardiologist stresses the importance of keeping the body parts moving, so I either take a long walk or ride my stationary bike if the weather is bad.

Soon there's the call from my wife to come to lunch. I always dry dishes and help clean up afterwards. Then I go through the dental routine again.

Now it's time to go out into the yard and pick up a little. In the summer, I skim leaves off the pool or possibly backwash the pool.

Sometime during the afternoon, I take a look at one of the many magazines I've subscribed to over so many years and seldom had time to read in the past.

I've got to watch *Jeopardy and Crossfire* after dinner and then try to stay awake until it's time for a bath before going to bed.

I'm sure glad I don't have to go to work for a living. I just wouldn't have time for all that anymore.

IT'S TIME TO COOK THEIR GOOSE

Pascack Valley Community Life
December 9, 1992

I first encountered Canada geese some years ago on a fairway of the Blue Hills County Club in Rockland. The geese, flying south, gazed longingly downward and must have thought, "That fairway looks like a peachy place to roost, multiply – and hang around."

My golfing partner said, "Put your boots on; we're going to wander through the Canada geese and all their endeavors to fertilize the earth."

Since then, the Canada geese have spread their good works throughout Bergen County. When they were getting ready to make their trek southward, a couple of leaders of the pack didn't want to overlook Bergen County when deciding upon a winter home. They must have felt it was better than Florida.

Now they've taken over lake areas, parks and everywhere there's a golf course or body of water. They regularly take a stab at my backyard pool but I chase them like a banshee with a broom.

West Point had them for a short period of time, but now they're gone. I'm afraid it will remain "Top Secret" how they did it.

The geese are indeed a problem. A friend of mine told me she recently got off a rare long drive at a golf course and the ball landed with a "plup". There was no roll at all to the ball. She wondered out loud, "Why don't we show some real, genuine concern for the homeless? We could cook the geese and serve them to all those poor, homeless people."

The 1918 law that established Canada geese as an endangered species certainly doesn't make any sense today. Millions of them must have been bred in Bergen County alone by now.

Perhaps, we could get rid of that 1918 amnesty – and serve all those geese up on a platter. Gee, I wonder if any of those cadets are currently eating geese at West Point and think they're eating chicken.

We can show genuine concern for our fellow man, and solve this monumental problem of too much fertilizer that has become a nuisance. Those pesky Canada geese – I think it's time their goose is cooked!

If you like the concept, I'll modestly take a bow. If the SPCA, the Geese Lovers Association of American/Canada, etc., get up in arms – don't look at me. Blame my good friend who got no roll on her golf ball.

KEEP THE PARTS OF THE MACHINE MOVING

Pascack Valley Community Life
December 2, 1992

One of life's most fundamental rules is, you've got to keep the basic parts moving. The concept is endemic to the human body. It applies to machines and organizations. If one does not walk enough, engage in sports, and generally keep active, the heart and the rest of the body become lethargic. The quality of performance deteriorates and ultimately, the body breaks down.

I'm the fortunate beneficiary of one of medical science's miracles – a device, which aids the performance of the human body – specifically the heart. Regularly, the tiny machine is deliberately activated to assure that it's working and preventing the body parts from figuratively rusting.

The world revolves around this principle of need for regular activation. The joggers, the walkers, the tennis players and the golfers are graphic representations of society's answering this need.

Business organizations become stagnant, political parties diminish in their capability to win, and governments stumble and fall when they become stodgy and allow themselves to become complacent. New ideas, motivational management and vibrant activity are products of dynamic, innovative and stimulating enterprise.

Be mindful that both the heart and the mind have the same need for perennial arousal, excitement and goading to new plateaus of achievement.

Many smart people contend that our educational system has fallen into a too tender jog. The parts need some impellent to do better. The health insurance system is virtually moribund. It's really not jogging; it's not even walking – it's standing still, hoping nobody will notice that rigor mortis is setting in.

Some practitioners in my lifelong profession of law enforcement have wondered out loud if we have not been so imbued with the standard motto of "To serve and to protect" that we have, on occasion, been rather remiss in professional police behavior and efficient use of police resources. Government, in general, has been accused of being less than efficient because of absence of competition, profit motive and lack of apprehension over failure in business. The quality revolution is jolting the large corporations, the "mom-and-pop" shops and even government operations. Everybody in Pascack Valley is mindful of the atmosphere.

I don't think it's too soon to put an initial evaluation upon President Bush and his administration. History will surely judge him as a kind, gentleman who presided during one of history's all-time monumental events – the collapse of Communism. But governments, like the human body, are energized by the same fundamental postulate – you've got to keep the parts constantly active and moving.

A SIMPLE LESSON IN PAINTING – NAVY STYLE

Pascack Valley Community Life

November 25, 1992

Sometimes we all need a little guidance and steering in the right direction. I'll never forget the guidance I got when I enlisted in the US Navy.

They gave me a *Bluejackets' Manual* – 1940. It didn't matter that I was going into the Office of Naval Intelligence as an enlisted specialist. The Navy had its regulations. Every enlisted man must have a *Bluejackets' Manual*. It would guide the young recruit during his entire Navy career. It would furnish him with the answer to everything life could throw at him – on the bridge, on duty, off duty and on the town.

I'm overwhelmed at this stage in life to browse through the manual. The writers had to be a combination of the almighty, a PhD, Solomon – a personification of omniscience.

We were advised on how to handle a hammock, cleanliness, stowing clothes, respect for authority and punishments in the Navy. It explained how to salute the flag and handle boats and cars.

It spelled out the differences – in detail – between battleships and rowboats. It also served as a manual of arms.

The manual has information on heaving lines, fenders, anchors and flag signals. We learn about messes – that is, the system of eating – not messes one encounters in the children's bedrooms or on some Bergen County streets.

Of course, I read the manual after I enlisted in the Navy, and concluded, "This is too detailed and tough for me. I'm putting in for a Commission and lead these men – it couldn't be more difficult than conforming with the *Bluejackets' Manual*."

And you had better measure up – or else!

For example, under the section, "Application of paint", it said,

1. Hold the brush by the handle and not the stock. If thebrush is held by the stock, the hands become covered with paint.
2. Hold the brush at right angles to the surface, with the bristles only touching and lift it clear of the surface when starting the return stroke.
3. Do not completely fill the brush with paint.

And there were more specific instructions under 4, 5, 6, 7, 8, 9 and 10.

Last year I got my grandsons to paint the garage floor. How stupid I was! I should have first had them all read the *Bluejackets' Manual*.

Their hands were covered with paint. Their clothes were covered with paint. The paintbrush stock and handle were covered with paint. Under item 8, the *Bluejackets' Manual* clearly states, "Keep the paint in the pot well mixed while the work is proceeding." However, my grandsons didn't do that. There was paint everywhere but little on the floor or in the pot well mixed.

Yet at two bucks a man, I guess I didn't do so bad. And my grandsons reminded me of that fact. I guess they're reading the Wall Street Journal in school these days.

But this year, they were vastly improved – if only they wouldn't argue so much over who had what brushes, and who had the roller. Come to think of it, they didn't have rollers in 1940, and the old *Bluejackets' Manual* didn't cover that problem. Very important, nevertheless, it told the painters to "keep the paint in the pot well mixed". That alone would have helped a whole lot.

LIVING FOR TOMORROW – TODAY!

The Catholic Advocate
September 16, 1992

At the age of fifty-four, I physically came apart at the seams. I had diverticulitis, an intestinal operation, and a temporary colostomy. "It was all tied in with stress," my doctor said. I was a supervisory special agent with the Waterfront Commission of New York Harbor fighting crime.

I retired and accepted a nice, prestigious position as director of the Bergen County Police and Fire Academy. It was fulfilling, enjoyable and productive. We educated young men in their public safety specialities. Then came a heart attack and retirement.

Open heart surgery, six catheterizations, cardiac arrest in the middle of my hometown, a few electrophysiological tests, implantation of an automatic defibrillator, and a proper amount of prayers, took place during the ensuing years. It really wasn't all that bad, strange to relate. I traveled, vacationed, was devoid of pain (in the main) and marvel, in retrospect, at how well I did.

At sixty, I didn't think I'd reach sixty-five; at sixty-five, I didn't think I'd reach seventy; at seventy, I was sure I'd never reach seventy-five. I am now in my seventy-fifth year. How I wish I had the gift of prescience! I'd have asked for active duty in the Gulf War or taken lessons on the piano. I always wanted to be a Floyd Cramer, Roger Williams or Carmen Cavallaro.

In short, live as if tomorrow is *not your last day*. There may be many fine tomorrows you never thought you'd see the light of.

NO COUNTING ON YOUR TOES

The Star-Ledger
September 15, 1992

Didja know that the managers of New Jersey's school system recently made a move that will surely enable the students to score considerably higher this December when taking their High School Proficiency Tests? The students will be required to use calculators when they take the tests. Everybody will derive the happy feeling. And that's nice.

The students will be happy that they scored higher. The parents will be happy because they will think their children have really progressed in computational skills. And the managers of the New Jersey school system will be happy because they will have succeeded in kidding everyone that they have improved the computational skills of the children of the state.

I guess we're discussing heady stuff like methods application and computational skills. Heck, if the kid knows the method, he can use his calculator to balance his checkbook and do all those dreary, vocational computational jobs. The kid might even become an actuary. But what about a mistake when you don't have a calculator available? What about checking that bill at the restaurant?

I think the commissioners should tie up all loose ends by giving out little cards to all high school graduates (along with the diploma) with an 800 number listed upon it (the commissioner's number). In those many, frantic emergencies the recent graduate can put in a quick call, recite the costs of the steak, coffee, dessert and tax, and have someone available with a calculator at the 800 number. The guy at the other end of the 800 number better have a calculator because he might not be too good at computational skills either.

SENIORS NOT THE ONLY GROUP THAT NEEDS RE-TESTING

Community Life
June 10, 1992

The current public problem is whether automobile drivers over a certain advanced age should be required to be annually tested. The thought is that they should also be tested after being a driver-participant in an accident.

Their reflexes are severely impaired, we're told. At the age of seventy-four, I don't need to be sold too vigorously on the concept. There's undoubtedly some considerable merit in the approach.

Another bad group is composed of young female drivers. They're more frightening than a skunk let loose at an afternoon meeting of the Daughters of the American Revolution.

They're reckless, discourteous, nasty, oblivious of the law, and suffer a dangerous propensity towards a fat foot on the accelerator. They frequently drive with only one hand upon the steering wheel, while dangerously utilizing the other to give the finger. I don't know, however, how they can be effectively tested. They could be sneaky, while being tested, and feign driving like normal people do.

"I'm running for President on advice of my campaign manager, and that's all I've got to say."

GOOD OLD PORKY

Sunday Post
April 26, 1992

Dear Editor,

I've played around in politics now and then. I was a county campaign manager on a couple of occasions.

The wish of every political leader is to get vibrant candidates who will hustle around appearing at affairs, talking on TV and radio, ringing doorbells and getting their message out to the voters. "I'm my party's candidate and I want to discuss the issues with you," they proudly proclaim. If it's a primary election, they tell us why they are better suited than the others seeking the nomination.

An old sardonic friend of mine, who once headed up a county political organization, had his own concept about some of the political eager beavers who rush about presenting themselves to the voters.

He held that many of the candidates foisted upon the party should get a comfortable hammock and a good book and hide out in the backyard during the campaign period. The less people see them and hear them speak, the better their chances of election. A dearth of public campaigning, coupled with a prayer, is their best bet.

Speech and political campaigning are assuredly connected with progress in politics and life in general. But there are many times when silence is golden. Even Porky the pig knew the proper time to say, "That's all, folks." Many candidates are not as wise and perceptive as good old Porky.

Sincerely,

T

Sexual Harassment

Office Flirtations
"Let me get you straight. Your complaint is that none of the men in this office has ever sexually harassed you!"

©1991 The Star-Ledger. All rights reserved. Printed with permission.

THE FINE LINE OF OFFICE FLIRTATIONS

The Star-Ledger
October 28, 1991

Dear Editor,

As a young man, I certainly was no Casanova. Forty-five years ago, however, I did with considerable trepidation venture into a flirtation. She was one of the prettiest girls in the office where we both worked. Happily, she responded favorably.

Three daughters and six grandchildren later, I have some misgivings. I realize I was on the threshold of plunging into the horrible arena of sexual harassment. For, I admit, I was definitely resolved to try again if my first flirtation proved unsuccessful. Sexual harassment!

One never knows when he is traveling on a highway adjacent to a truck laden with dynamite.

Sincerely,

T

MORE DEADLY THAN THE DISEASE

The Star-Ledger
March 18, 1991

Dear Editor,

The new American dream is to die without being totally wiped out by medical bills.

Sincerely,

T

NOTHING TO SNEEZE ABOUT

The Record
February 3, 1986

Scientists claim to have come up with a drug that'll prevent the common cold. What a terrible setback to many aspects of the national economy!

Doctors, purveyors of aspirin, cough medicine, handkerchiefs, hot water bottles, and Mom's hot chicken soup will all suffer. So will the writers who monthly fill our favorite magazines with articles on ways to prevent colds. Many researchers at the major pharmaceutical houses may have to join the unemployment-insurance lines.

Advertising agencies that collect so much revenue from pushing ineffectual cold remedies will also bite the dust. Supermarkets will close whole sections. Think a little while, and you'll come up with many persons, places and things whose whole life is dependent upon the continued prevalence of the common cold.

Like everything in life, however, there is a positive side. Industrial and governmental employers will save untold billions of dollars each year from the precipitous drop in absenteeism. Efficiency should rise immensely, because employees won't be walking around sniffling, barking, blowing the nose, or taking trips to the lounge for a little rest.

Has anyone stopped to think about who will be the most adversely affected person in America? He is the ingenious, contriving malingerer.

Governmental employers and many private enterprises grant a certain number of sick days each year. Most public employees, including police officers and teachers, are entitled to ten days each year.

These days are intended to be used in an emergency. What emergency? An illness that prevents one's availability on the assembly line. Everyone has his own assembly line.

I know many old associates who ponder, around November each year, and come to a startling realization. "I have five unused sick days left!" This calls for a "fakeitis" day off from work.

"Maybe two days will look even better," they tell themselves. "The boss might think I'm really sick."

The adroit phone call is made. Amidst sneezing (this is easily simulated) and a few horrible coughs into the boss' ear, one explains how he's come down with a wicked cold. I had one nasty boss who used to say, "I believe you, just don't cough in my ear."

I sure am glad that I'm retired. The game is up for many of us skilled fakers. The "fakeitis" day will be a thing of the past.

Maybe we could devise a new reason for staying home – like an attack of nerves. The researchers will need quite a while to cure that one.

PLAYING INSURANCE GAMES

The Record
December 27, 1984

You had some medical problems, and you're going to submit your hospitalization claims for payment? Hold your hat. Get ready for an ulcer, a heart attack, or a nervous breakdown.

Our health-insurance system is a hodgepodge of mass confusion, waste and inefficiency, all designed to confound the insured.

The word is that Medicare is going broke, and the prices for private insurance are soaring out of reach. One wonders why. The companies under this mad-hatter system endeavor to pay no claims. They delay, refuse, or demand another form until the insured gives up or becomes a statistic in the mortality tables.

My elderly sister recently exhibited to me a pile of insurance rejections for specious reasons.

"This has me so confused, I'm going to forget it," she said. "I don't know what in the world they're talking about."

She isn't alone. How many claims of elderly and uninformed persons go down the drain in this manner? I'm confused, too – and I once taught insurance courses at Rutgers University.

One has to develop a sense of humor, for the system is indeed ghoulishly hilarious.

I've received a reply – with attendant delay – tied to a request for my doctor's identification number. Don't forget to fill in all the spaces. I received one claim back because the sex wasn't checked on a form for my wife, Helene. Helene is a she.

One of the old faithfuls for delay is to credit the claimant with the amount towards the deductible, which has to be met before any cash is shelled out.

"But," you complain, "the deductible was met five months

Hurdles Of Health Insurance Claims

221

ago, and you've made several cash payments in the interim."

"Ooops, I guess you're right. But make copies of the forms that indicate the deductible was met and forward them to us."

You always have to send copies of the company's forms back to them, confirming what you discussed on the phone. More pieces of paper.

"No payment has been made on this claim. Submit it to the federal Black Lung and Workers Compensation Agency in Washington, DC, and then resubmit if the whole claim is not paid."

What? I never worked in the mines. I've had a heart attack – I think these people helped it along. And I've had an intestinal operation – I think they contributed to that, too. But never black lung.

"Ooops, I guess we made another mistake. Send us a copy of the form indicating what you just said."

now should hear about the approach of the insurance industry to the "head of the family". My daughter works for the state, and one of the benefits of her employment is good insurance benefits. There's that wonderful coverage through Blue Cross and Blue Shield as primary insurers and Prudential as major-medical provider.

But since her husband also has coverage, he's arbitrarily designated as head of the family. All claims on the two children and him have to be submitted to his insurance carrier (also Blue Cross and Blue Shield). But since his is a small-group plan, it pays only for frostbite that's contracted in Panama City at high noon.

Nevertheless, his wife is thereby sentenced to untold travail in order to receive indemnification on her insurance. She has to submit to Blue Cross–Blue Shield under her husband's policy, get a rejection, and then submit to her own Blue Cross–Blue Shield coverage and get a rejection. Finally, she can submit to Prudential under major medical and receive a payment. At this juncture, the doctor is disgusted with filling out new forms.

This is our private hospitalization system, which is allegedly running on all eight cylinders with no knocks or squealing bearings. The squealing you hear is the insured, who's completely exasperated. You can anticipate an error on half of your claims these days.

If you're ready for another visit to the doctor for nerves, ulcers, or a thumping headache, brace yourself when the woman on the phone tells you sweetly that it will be about six weeks before you get the refund that resulted from the insurance company's foul-up. You've already waited six weeks. Six weeks is, for some reason, the favorite number. Try not to get too excited if it extends into six months.

The companies say their concern for our welfare is proven by their new toll-free phone numbers. They save us the cost of paying to follow-up upon their many errors. If you're retired, it isn't too bad. You may take all morning to get through, but hell, you have little else to do.

Don't expect the insurance people to answer a broad range of questions. They just tell you about the handling of your claim. Call the regional office if you want more information, they say. Here you'll be dutifully referred to the main office.

Hold your temper at this point, for you shouldn't be surprised if the voice at the main office tells you she really can't answer that question either. Be ready for a long pause while she determines where to refer you.

My sister might have been right. Maybe it is better just to forget it. If this gets you too excited, you could become a candidate for one of Vander Plaat's funeral homes.

*Since writing this article, the system has admittedly materially changed. It's monumentally *worse*.

THE REAL LIVE *ON THE WATERFRONT*

Illinois Police Officer

Summer 1984

On the Waterfront, the motion picture, was shown again on television recently. It is a classic film with stars including Marlon Brando, Eva Maria Saint, Lee J Cobb, Karl Malden and Rod Steiger, and it was no great surprise when it won the Academy Award as the outstanding picture of the year.

The book and the movie came on the scene not too long after completion of the investigations by the Kefauver Committee, the New York State Crime Commission and the New Jersey Law Enforcement Counsel. The New York State Crime Commission, particularly, spelled out a life of crime and violence on the docks of New York and New Jersey. Wally Aluetto and Francis Kelly had been murdered in short order in Hoboken, tied in with control of the Hoboken piers – and all that went with it. "Charley the Jew" Yanowski had been ice-picked to death with twenty-five or thirty jabs of the ice-pick. He was then left hanging from a longshoreman's hook on a fence of a New Jersey schoolyard. "Cockeye" Dunn shot a man dead on assignment in connection with North River intrigue – but he shot the wrong guy by mistake.

Names in the news were known to anyone who read as far as page two in the newspapers. They were "Tough Tony" Anastasia, Alex DiBrizzi, Mickey Bowers, "Keffie", "Machine Gun" Campbell, Ed Albert Ackalitis, Mike Clemente, Nick Maschucci, Pat Ferrone, "Joe the Gent" Giantomassi, "Ding Ding" Bell, his brother Buster, who later went to jail participating in the jury fix at the famous Jimmy Hoffa trial – and many more. Lurking in the background, authorities claimed the string pullers were Albert

Anastasio, Vito Genovese, Jerry Catena, Carlo Gambino, Tony Bender, Eddie McGrath, and *gentlemen* of equal stature.

The New York State Crime Commission spelled out a litany of crimes including murder, gambling, large-scale thievery, kick-backs, loan-sharking, labor payoffs by industry and atrocious assaults. You name it. Father John M Corridon became famous through his crusade against waterfront crime. The New York State Crime Commission and the New Jersey Law Enforcement Counsel jointly recommended that a bi-state commission be formed to eradicate the vacuum in law enforcement that existed on the piers of the world's greatest harbor.

I was one of an initially small group of men recruited from the Federal Bureau of Investigation, Office of Naval Intelligence, New York District Attorney Frank Hogan's office, the old Federal Narcotics Bureau, and the New Jersey State Police. We were to serve as the nucleus group to confront waterfront crime head on at the Port of New York Harbor. In the meantime, Budd Schulberg's book *Waterfront* had become a national success, and the film industry was in the process of making *On The Waterfront* in Hoboken when I was assigned to Hoboken as a special agent for the newly created Waterfront Commission of New York Harbor. Jimmy Petrosino, who discovered the money in the Bruno Hauptman garage in connection with the Lindberg baby kidnapping case, was one of our original groups. Another pioneer was the late Eugene Haussling, a former New Jersey State Police lieutenant, who had headed up the Bergen County gambling probe and investigation of the Willie Moretti murder.

I have felt an affinity to the movie, *On The Waterfront*, from the day of my assignment to Hoboken. It is generally known that Budd Schulberg's major source material was the hearings conducted by the New York State Crime Commission. Experts familiar with the waterfront can name the prototypes for most of the main characters in the book. They were depicted in the book by Schulberg. We were investigating some of them while the movie was being filmed.

At the very time the filming was taking place in Hoboken, a protracted and vicious strike had broken out on the piers throughout New York and New Jersey. The old-line International

Longshoremen's Association had been expelled from the house of labor by the American Federal of Labor, because it was alleged to be dominated by "the mob". A rival union was formed, the International Longshoremen's Association – American Federation of Labor. Paul Hall, former president of the Seafarers International Union, threw his weight behind the new union. The two unions were pitted in a death struggle awaiting the jurisdictional election by the National Labor Relations Board to determine the collective bargaining agent. Brother was often pitted against brother-in-law amid the hurling of bricks, rioting and utilization of baseball bats. We worked from sunup until late into the night covering riots, assaults and threats. The Commission worked with all the NJ police departments in an endeavor to control turbulence on the piers. Longshoremen on the North River threw marbles under the horses to lessen their effectiveness, which brought forth swinging clubs by the police. On several days when large rioting was rumored at Fort Newark, New Jersey, the Port of New York–New Jersey Authority sent a veritable army of its police to aid us in confronting the chaos. Here and there, the ILA–AFL men would get on to piers and work them. But it was generally accomplished in the middle of flailing fists, prancing mounted patrols and flying rocks.

And all the time, the movie cameras were grinding in Hoboken. They needed many extras for the film to portray what was indeed happening in real life all around us. Longshoremen worked together as extras on the picture and threw punches at each other at the morning call for gangs and during the day and night when other crises took place.

The men associated with the ILA–AFL were friendly to the commission but the ILA–Independent men represented the enemy to us. When *On The Waterfront* is replayed on late shows, I often watch it out of nostalgia. I see men on the screen who were the enemy; many of them I later became friendly with when the NLRB vote determined the collective bargaining agent. And strangely, the men voted for the old union, the ILA–Independent. I also see men who had been associated with the ILA–AFL who were sources of information to me in the real-life, explosive drama that was taking place on the docks.

Elia Kazan, the director, wanted a number of rugged-looking individuals to play the parts of union henchmen assistants to the union boss, Johnny Friendly (Lee J Cobb). He gathered together a number of famous retired prizefighters and wrestlers such as Tony Galento, Tami Mauriello, the Angel and others to play the parts. However, mingling with the famous fighters and wrestlers, I recognized a longshoreman from the area. He had fought locally, had his nose pushed in, and fitted in very well with the famous individuals who were playing the roles of tough union officials. He was friendly with me on the piers – when not playing his role of a tough guy in the movie. Tony Mike DeVencenzo was also friendly with me, having been associated with the ILA–AFL. He sued the motion picture company, complaining that it was he they portrayed in the role Marlon Brando played. Tony Mike had been a fighter. So was Terry Malloy (is it significant that initials are the same?), the role Marlon Brando played. "Tony Mike" flew pigeons as a hobby and so did Terry Malloy in the picture. "Tony Mike" had a relation who owned a bakery shop. So did Terry Malloy. "Tony Mike" ultimately decided to testify before the Crime Commission against Ed Florio and his friends. Terry Malloy also decided to testify against the mob. "Tony Mike" sued and got a settlement.

Others did not sue. Waterfront crime watchers, however, almost unanimously agreed that Johnny Friendly was based upon the real life Ed Florio. When Florio got out of jail, my partners and I were watching him in his car coming out of the self-same alley used for scenes in *On The Waterfront*. In the movie, Johnny Friendly's second man was ultimately ice-picked to death and hung on a fence with a longshoreman's hook – just like "Charley the Jew". In real life, however, I was told Charley the Jew was second man to nobody. He was indeed a piece of work. The priest in *On The Waterfront* was undoubtedly Father Corridon.

Recently, it has been announced that Telly Savalas of Kojak fame is due to perform in *Waterfront* on the New York stage. It is also based on the Budd Schulberg book. We'll see the whole panorama again. I'll surely go to see it. I'll recognize many of the persons the actors will be portraying. But I will not see the men who appeared in the background of the movie. They were the real *living thing* who doubled as extras in the motion picture and in real life performed as longshoremen and checkers on the docks during the chilling activities which were taking place daily. It all happened many years ago when we were acting out a turbulent, live rendition of life on the waterfront. Filming of the picture was a happening that took place concurrently with our dodging horses and bricks, while many of the men were engaged in two different worlds – motion picture acting and waterfront reality.

A GRAND GUESSING GAME
Exclusionary Rule On Evidence Puts Police In A Bind

The Record

August 15, 1983

America has long been enchanted by guessing games – on TV, in newspapers, even in the mail. But what's the trillion-dollar champion guessing game of all? You'll never guess, but it's America's criminal-justice system.

US Supreme Court Justice Benjamin Cardozo predicted nearly fifty years ago, "The criminal is to go free, because the constable has blundered." His comment referred to the 1914 decision in *Weeks vs United States*, in which the Supreme Court declared that evidence obtained in violation of the Constitution's Fourth Amendment is not admissible in federal prosecutions.

But the exclusionary rule is a judicially created rule of law. It's not included in the Fourth Amendment. It's nowhere in the Constitution or the federal criminal code. We didn't inherit it from English law. We are, in fact, the only civilized nation in the world that requires the exclusion of such evidence.

Since 1961, the exclusionary rule has been extended to all state as well as federal prosecutions. The effect has been exactly as Justice Cardozo predicted.

The purpose of the exclusionary rule was to deter improper police conduct. It was an example of engaging in the frequent modern judicial practice of legislating from the bench.

As Harvard Professor James Q Wilson has said, "No officer is punished when the exclusionary rule is invoked. Rather, the prosecution's case is lost. If a guilty person goes free because of improperly collected evidence that would have established his guilt is excluded, then the victim of the crime, and society at large, bear the costs of the police error."

What's most disconcerting, the invocation of the exclusionary rule results in the freeing of so many patently guilty criminals. This happens whether the officer is acting in good faith or not.

Disturbing, too, is the conclusion of an exhaustive study done by the American Bar Foundation that announced, "Today, more than fifty years after the exclusionary rule was adopted for the federal courts... there is still no convincing evidence to verify the factual premise of deterrence upon which the rule is based."

Chief Justice Burger has also noted, "There is no empirical evidence to support the claim (that) the rule deters illegal conduct of law-enforcement officials."

Most deplorably, the exclusionary rule has given the nation a mammoth guessing game. It has created a horrendous guessing game for police officers and it has afflicted the judicial system with a never-ending guessing game over what the exclusionary rule really means and whether it's constitutional.

The police officer must ponder on the law when deciding what avenues to pursue when making an arrest. He's to think about it while endeavoring to protect the evidence and himself.

The police officer very often has to make these decisions while he's pursuing a car at 80 mph or when the suspect is beginning his move for a weapon or attempting to flee with the evidence.

But truthfully – just what is the police officer really doing at that crucial moment when he's earning his pay? As a reasonable man, he's guessing about the procedure to follow and he's guessing what line of reasoning the judges will take.

When the case gets to the courts, what are the judges' postures? They're not in the 80 mph car pursuing the suspect, nor are they standing out there determining whether to use a gun. They're sitting in their chambers reading the law, mulling over it in tranquility, trying to come up with the proper legal decision.

But they're also engaged in America's grandest guessing game. And the moral well being of a nation is riding on these guesses.

Justice William Rehnquist has said that the exclusionary rule "unrealistically requires that policemen investigating serious crimes make no errors whatever." This has placed an impossible restriction on police officers.

This was clearly seen in two drug cases, *New York vs Belton* and *Robbins vs California*. In both cases, police officers lawfully stopped a car, smelled burned marijuana, located marijuana in the passenger compartment of the car and legally arrested the occupants.

In the *Robbins* case, the officer then found two packages wrapped in green paper in a recessed compartment of the car, opened them without a warrant, and found thirty pounds of marijuana. In the *Belton* case, an officer found a jacket in the passenger compartment, unzipped the pocket without a warrant, and found a quantity of cocaine.

The Supreme Court ultimately asked both sides to address whether *Robbins* should be reconsidered. The court did so because, in *Belton* and *Robbins*, three justices held both searches legal. Three justices held both illegal. The three justices who controlled the final decision found the *Robbins* search illegal but the *Belton* search legal. In its 1982 decision in *United States vs Ross*, the court reconsidered the holdings in the *Robbins* case and determined the search legal.

In their journeys through state and federal courts, the *Robbins*, *Belton*, and *Ross* cases resulted in a most perplexing scorecard. In these three cases, there were thirty votes (decisions) that at least one of the searches was unlawful, but thirty-four that at least one of the searches was lawful.

Pity the poor police officer guessing which direction he should pursue while guessing how he thinks the courts will guess.

It's my judgment that the present construction of the exclusionary rule will have to be changed. The evidence should stand. But genuine punitive action must be devised for penalizing the police officer who deliberately violates the law.

Justice Cardozo's dire prediction should not continue to be a reality. Let's leave the guessing games to TV and the newspapers. The police officer is an unfair target. His discomfort is also the discomfort of society.

GONE FISHING

Dear Editor,

I'm no Isaak Walton. I should affirm that I really don't know how to fish. In the words of that renowned philosopher Gomer Pyle – "That's for dang sure."

As a kid, one of my buddies sold me on visiting the pretty Hudson County Park Lake in New Jersey to fish. He had caught a gold fish there. I was bubbling with excitement and I yearned to also catch a gold fish. In later years, the officials at the helm in North Bergen, NJ, changed the name of the park to Braddack Park in honor of my old neighbor Jimmy Braddack. He was once the heavyweight champion of the world. Jimmy made a big mistake. He fought Joe Louis. He was no longer the champ after the fourth round. As a former champ, however, he rated a park being named after him. The lake was no champion, however, in yielding up gold fish – any fish.

My mistake was to have gone fishing in the lake. On that occasion, and a few more, I never caught a gold fish. I never caught "a fish". I never got a bite. It rather soured me on fishing.

Years later, however, I visited the Pennsylvania farm of my wife's successful young nephew. The graceful country atmosphere of his farm is enhanced by three ponds, two of which are kept stocked with fish. I fished there. How can one say "no" when graciously handed a fishing rod and a bunch of worms?

I fished off a little float attached to the land. Our host unfortunately hadn't gotten around to having proper buoyancy attached to the float. To my amazement, I hooked a fish which dragged my bobber under the surface of the water signaling a powerful catch – beyond a doubt. I loudly and elatedly hollered out, "I've hooked one! I've caught a fish." My little fishing companion rushed onto the float, came to my side and leaned over to cheerfully view my monumental catch in the making.

It was like being on the AKA 84 (*Waukesha*) at Okinawa during World War II. We were unloading heavy cargo onto a very large barge. In opposition to a Chief Warrant Officer's sage advice, the Executive Officer insisted upon putting one last heavy draft of cargo onto the barge. The barge instantaneously flipped to the side far enough to dump the entire load into Buckner Bay and righted itself in a fraction of a second's time.

It was exactly the same with my little fishing partner and me. The float flipped to the side and quickly dumped my partner, my fishing rod and me into the pond. Happily, the water was only waist high. I frantically but quickly saw to the safety of my pretty little partner. I then fetched my rod and climbed ashore.

A handsome little fish was surprisingly still flitting around – hooked to my rod and line. That settled it conclusively. I would definitely never pursue the hobby of fishing. If you have to go through an experience like that to catch a fish, I wanted no part of it. I'm not that good a swimmer and might not encounter shallow water the next time around. Fishing's most definitely out. I'll read, walk and jerk around with various forms of leisure occupation – but no fishing. Isaak Walton – it's all yours.

Sincerely,

T

POP'S BAD MANNERS

Dear Editor,

With old age, one should be admonished to guard against forming bad propensities – crude habits, for one.

I found that superannuated people have a great disposition to pass wind. It's called flatulence. I'm assured I'm not alone with this conclusion. It seems to be so much more prevalent than it used to be in our youth. My wife bridles. I contend that the multiplicity of medical drugs might be a factor. Another is the diminution in physical activity. Parts of the body are not sufficiently active. My wife argues that these are merely specious excuses. The answer, she says, is "Don't do it."

I was eating breakfast the other day and had the urge and the impelling need. It rattled its way into audibility with a crescendo via the wooden seat of the kitchen chair. My wife, in alarm, inquired, "What was that?" I said, "I think it was a truck backfiring." She quickly looked out of the window, saw no truck, then disdainfully said, "That was no truck, that was you – that's disgusting."

The other day, I had another occasion. It wasn't nearly as audible but one of my loveable grandsons smilingly turned informant and proclaimed to the world, "Pop farted." My wife angrily said, "That foul word is not even in the dictionary – and as for you, that's a horrible example for your grandchildren." I innocently commented, "There's a happy aspect to it all. When I hear that, I know I'm still alive. She acidly responded, "When I hear that, I think you're nuts."

With long living together, divergent opinions often arise. It's to be expected. It's really normalcy. Crudity, I must admit, is often an unwelcome gift of old age – and it is indeed lamentable. Wives agree. Children wink and smile.

Sincerely,

T

ARTICULATION THROUGH KEEPING ONE'S MOUTH SHUT

Community Life

There's a lot in favor of shutting one's mouth instead of constantly holding court.

Yes indeed! For many years, we have read and heard about the glib young men who have progressed onward and upward in the business and political worlds. We're told "They're good on their feet."

The suave spellbinder is the envy of everyone in the room – the room where he is performing like a combination of William Jennings Bryan, Lee Iacocca and John F Kennedy. It seems success is almost always equated with one's ability to speak well.

I know of many friends who die a thousand deaths prior to attending an important social event. Will they be able to fluently take part in the kind of smart, profound conversation which generally takes place?

Admittedly, some people don't say enough at social gatherings but one must keep in mind that sophisticated conversation is frequently not profundity. It's verbosity. A friend of mine used to call it wind jamming.

While some people don't say enough but say it well, many say too much and say it badly. An old professor of mine in college once said, "There is a good case for the strong, silent man." A lot of men in industry earn their reputations based on infrequent but relevant commentaries. In between, they may not know what the conversation is all about, but they have the good sense to say nothing. When one opens his mouth, he frequently confirms how little he knows.

PIPE SMOKERS DON'T GET LOCKED UP!

The Bulletin

May–June 1967

Pipe smokers don't get locked up. Well – hardly ever.

While on a pilferage patrol along the New York City waterfront several years ago, my partner and I were sitting upon a stakeout where longshoremen had been reported to have been running away with liquor cargo. Shortly after having commenced the surveillance of the area, we observed a longshoreman hurrying across the street in the direction of the location where the thieves were reported to have been depositing their loot. We watched him closely to observe whether there were any bulges in his coat pockets when suddenly Pete Ozelski, my partner, commented – "He's alright, he's a pipe smoker. Pipe smokers never get locked up." He proceeded to state that he never locked up a pipe smoker during better than twenty years of assignment as a detective with the New York City Police Department.

It set me to wondering. I don't recall having locked up any pipe smokers during my career with the Office of Naval Intelligence and later with the Waterfront Commission of New York Harbor. I have spoken to many detectives and special agents since Mr. Ozelski's revelation and they agree.

It's unfortunate that the FBI does not publish statistics on how many pipe smokers are arrested during the course of a year. The FBI's annual report contains a breakdown by cities, bank robbers, kidnappers, thefts from interstate commerce, males, females, age brackets and others – but nothing about pipe smokers. And I think it's regrettable, for very possibly, it would reveal the amazing empirical conclusion that the steady, complacent suckers upon pipe-stems are our best citizens. The various federal and state commissions which are being currently formed to determine the causes of crime and our best approaches for facing up to ubiquitous crime might do well to suggest starting a campaign to get everyone puffing upon a corncob or a fine old English briar.

My father-in-law is an inveterate pipe smoker and he's the kind of man who would advertise in the local newspaper if he were to find a wallet – and he'd undoubtedly sequester any funds found in the wallet for an indefinite period on the contingency that the poor unfortunate who lost it might show up some day.

Employers, however, might not look kindly upon an anti-crime crusade predicated upon an educational program to get all citizens on the pipe. For pipe smokers generally appear to smoke matches rather than tobacco. They are constantly in the process of lighting the pipe, which certainly must detract from productivity on the job.

Let's sit back for a few moments and look more closely at this premise that pipe smokers make good citizens. The kindly old professor is always a pipe smoker – is he not? A Conan Doyle's famous crimebuster, Sherlock Holmes, devoted his considerable talents to solving the case of the Red Headed League, the Tripoff Murder, the Atkinson Brothers case and ever so many other perplexing confrontations with breaking the law. He did his best thinking while seated in his apartment at Baker Street with a black clay pipe in his mouth. His inseparable companion, Dr. Watson, also poked tobacco into a friendly pipe while he discussed cases with the brilliant Holmes.

In the moving pictures – and in real life – who is the perennial villain? He is the bookie on the corner or the murderer-for-hire who, in a most sinister manner, puffs upon a cigarette and usually pitches it into the gutter – a litterbug to boot – before he embarks upon his nasty business of assault, murder or terrorizing some poor old lady.

And what about the cigar smoker? Is he not the crooked politician who takes your taxes and mine and misappropriates them to his own selfish desires – all the time puffing upon a big, fat, obnoxious, cheap smelling cigar? He is also the big time racketeer who is in charge of the nasty cigarette smoker alluded to above, who executes the illicit deeds on behalf of the "rope smoking boss". When the cigarette smoking hoods succeed in life they become cigar smokers – but never pipe smokers.

Once in a while in the moving pictures, you will recall that the suave, courteous, pipe smoking individual such as Lionel Atwell or Boris Karloff popped up as the surprise villain. Observe if you will, however, that this is always in the nature of the O'Henry surprise ending. For the moving picture producers also know that pipe smokers are normally not villains.

Possibly, the very functional nature of pipe smoking contributes to good citizenship. You need a pipe, a pouch and several pockets full of matches to properly experience the exquisite joys of smoking a pipe. It may be that their hands are so constantly engaged with holding the pipe, shifting the pouch, grabbing for matches, lighting the matches and emptying the charred ashes from the pipe, that one never has time to place one's hands upon contraband, the fair lady's neck or a gun to effect the holdup. It is basic in crime circles that one needs two free hands to use when stealing the hot stove. Then, too, the pipe smoker's pockets are so filled with matches, pouch or pipe that there is just no place to hide many forms of ill-gotten loot. So, functionally, he may be the good citizen through necessity.

Whatever the reason, however, I'm sure Sherlock Holmes would have confirmed my premise and the secret files of the FBI, if permitted to be researched in this direction, would confirm – pipe smokers never get locked up. Well, hardly ever, said Boris Karloff as he took a deep draw upon his pipe and, with the other hand, sneaked the poison pill into the kind old lady's coffee.